LIVING WISDOM
OF THE FAR NORTH

Tales and Legends from Chukotka and Alaska

By Alexander B. Dolitsky

Illustrated by Tamara Semenova & Leigh Rust

Published by
Alaska-Siberia Research Center, Juneau, Alaska
Copyright ©AKSRC 2011 • Publication No. 16

First edition
Published by the Alaska-Siberia Research Center,
P.O. Box 34871, Juneau, Alaska, U.S.A. 99803.
www.aksrc.org

Jacket illustrations by Tamara Semenova and Leigh Rust

Printed and bound by Amica, Inc.
Printed in China

General editor: Alexander B. Dolitsky
Copy editor of the English text: Liz Dodd
Proofreaders of the English text: Fred Andresen, Willis Longyear, and Mark Kissel
Proofreaders of the Russian text: Ilya Grinberg and Masha Ziering
Illustrators: Tamara Semenova and Leigh Rust
Translators: Alexander B. Dolitsky, Henry N. Michael, and James F. Gebhardt
Consultants: Alexander B. Dolitsky, Wallace Olson, and Azat Mamedinov
Book designer: Shannon Bodie, Lightbourne, Inc.
Jacket designer: Shannon Bodie, Lightbourne, Inc.

Hardback edition: ISBN: 978-0-9653891-8-1

Key words: Tales, Legends, North, Yupik, Chukchi, Siberia, Alaska

CONTENTS

FOREWORD

Living Wisdom of the Far North: Tales and Legends from Chukotka and Alaska compiles several traditional oral stories of the aboriginal peoples of the Russian and North American Far North and includes two new stories created in the spirit of those traditions.

I wrote two literary fables for this edition, "How Swan Found Happiness" and "The Quarrel between Sun and Moon," incorporating the style and motifs found in the northern oral narratives. Like many of the traditional tales compiled in this volume, the purpose of these two stories is to explain, to teach, and to exemplify how to behave in society. My two tales do not provide an authoritative code by which to live, but they do express a moral directive in imploring readers to examine the extent to which we humans are victims of circumstances versus the extent to which we are the makers of our own destiny.

While written in a traditional style, my tales contain lessons relevant to today's social and political challenges, such as regional conflicts and territorial disputes, displacement of people from their homelands to foreign lands, adaptation to new social and physical environments, and the search for happiness and peace in the turbulent and ethnically diverse global society in which we now find ourselves. In other words, how we might begin to get along with one another and understand, respect, and tolerate our neighbors' traditions, beliefs, customs, accents, and rights, while at the same time preserving our own unique ethnic identities and cultural values.

In addition to these two original tales, I have selected four out of 59 Siberian Yupik Eskimo stories and four out of 67 Chukchi tales that I previously edited and compiled in two separate volumes in 1997[1] and 2000,[2] after Henry N. Michael, an authority on Siberian anthropology, had translated the volumes from Russian into English. In those volumes, the indigenous tales were not customized nor adapted by the editor, but set forth as spoken by Siberian Yupik and Chukchi orators and recorded by Soviet ethnographers in the early twentieth century. Eight of the indigenous stories in this book were adapted from Russian translations of those recordings, which were later translated into English.

---

1 Dolitsky, Alexander B. and Henry N. Michael, *Fairy Tales and Myths of the Bering Strait Chukchi*. Juneau: Alaska-Siberia Research Center, Publication No. 9, 1997.

2 Dolitsky, Alexander B. and Henry N. Michael, *Tales and Legends of the Yupik Eskimos of Siberia*. Juneau: Alaska-Siberia Research Center, Publication No. 11, 2000.

At each stage of translating the texts—from their original Siberian Yupik and Chukchi renditions into Russian, and then from Russian into English—the translators and editor have sought to preserve each speaker's voice within the limitations of Russian and English grammatical and stylistic norms. Factors such as the era surrounding the recording, the skill, age, and literacy of the narrator, and the genre of the work strongly influenced the form and content of the original written text. Indeed, any modern iteration of these tales, whether spoken, or, as in this volume, written, cannot help but vary from the oral narratives of pre-literate Siberian Yupik and Chukchi speakers recorded over a hundred years ago.

The stories of the aboriginal peoples of the Chukchi Peninsula and Alaska provide a window through which one can glimpse, across time, not only the ideology, customs, and beliefs of the Siberian Yupik and Chukchi peoples, but also geological and historical events and the particulars of everyday life that shaped their economy and core values, which in turn shaped their cultural traditions.

The oral narratives of the Siberian Yupik and Chukchi may be categorized into the following main genres:

1. *Myths, magical tales, and legends* serving three primary functions: (a) cosmogonical explanations for the origin of the universe; (b) magical tales dealing with tribal identity and man's struggle against evil; and (c) legends surrounding shamanic journeys. In this volume, "The Two Strongmen and the Oldster" falls into the genre of a magical tale, and "The Mouse and the Mountain" may be categorized as a legend.

2. *Heroic tales* dedicated to the struggles of strong and brave people, often against strangers from another tribe or other offenders. "The Woman with the Ball," "The Formation of the Strait," and "Akannykay—Bad Antlers" represent heroic tales in this edition.

3. *Economic and domestic tales* describing ordinary situations in the realm of everyday life. In these stories, fantasy yields to a realistic description of living conditions. In a fight with tricksters and oppressors, rather than being helped by magical forces or mythical transformations, the protagonist prevails by being clever, resourceful, physically superior, and courageous.

4. *Totemic tales, myths, and legends* wherein cultural heroes take the forms of animals, birds, and insects often engaged in the search for food. These anthropomorphized characters conduct their housekeeping in human-like dwellings, sometimes dressed in human clothing, and often assisted in their quest for food by such human accessories as hunting gear, reindeer, and boats. "The Raven and the Owl," "The Smart Vixen and the Teals," "The Mouse and the Marmot," and "Akannykay—Bad Antlers" all exemplify this kind of tale.

How Swan Found Happiness

These principal genres of Siberian Yupik and Chukchi folklore closely resemble the functions of the folklore of the indigenous peoples of the Russian and American Far North with whom the Siberian Yupik and Chukchi have had longstanding cultural ties. Interaction among the northern cultures is directly reflected in the development and existence of the oral traditions of the Chukotka and Alaska aborigines, whose stories were preserved in both Siberian Yupik Eskimo and Chukchi folklore.

Characters, motifs, and plot elements shared across cultures oftentimes communicate different lessons, however. For example, Aesop, the ancient Greek author of classical fables (ca. 620-564 B.C.E.), told the story of the ants and a grasshopper. In this tale, the ants work hard putting away food for the winter, while the grasshopper enjoys the sun and creates musical sounds. When winter comes, the ants reject the grasshopper's request for food, admonishing him for being lazy and failing to secure a sufficient supply to sustain himself over the forthcoming harsh winter. The Japanese have a similar story, but, in their version, when winter comes, the ants all welcome and help the other insect because he entertained them while they worked in the summer.

Readers may find a similar dynamic at play in some of the northern folktales and legends, where stories share common characters and genres, but the events in the tale ultimately are interpreted in a different way, leading to a different moral.

In this edition, each story is set out in both Russian and English, not only to make the story available to Russian readers, but also for the purpose of providing a comparative study of the effects of each language's writing conventions on the oral narratives. As is evident from the linguistic variations found in the side-by-side English and Russian versions printed in this volume, different punctuation and other grammatical rules influence each written rendition of the old oral narrative, which, in turn, influences the voice in which the reader "hears" the story told.

I have designed this volume with four groups of readers in mind: first, young children who like an engaging picture story; second, young adult readers interested in deepening their intercultural understanding of circumpolar traditions and Far North lifestyles; third, English-speaking students of the Russian language and Russian-speaking students of the English language; and, finally, ethnographers, academicians, and others seeking to engage with the oral folk creations of the Far North in order to learn more about not only that area's geography and geographic origins, its cultures, and its historical events, but also some of the issues surrounding the recording and modern day written presentation of its indigenous tales.

For their useful comments and constructive suggestions, I would like to express my thanks to Miriam G. Lancaster, Fred Andresen, Ilya Grinberg, Dianne Holmes, Dr. Charles Holmes, Masha Ziering, Martin Niemi, Elena Farkas, Willis Longyear, Liz Dodd, Jay Brodrick, Wally Olson, Timothy Fraychineaud, Mark Kissel, Raandi Miller, Azat Mamedinov, and my daughter Elena A. Dolitsky.

This edition is dedicated to a group of visionary and prominent Alaskans: Ernest Gruening, William A. Egan, Theodore F. Stevens, Walter J. Hickel, Jay S. Hammond, Elizabeth W. Peratrovich, Thomas B. Stewart, John Binkley, Susan Butcher, Elmer Rasmuson, Fran Ulmer, Rie Munoz, and Jon Van Zyle.

ETHNOGRAPHIC INFORMATION

Siberian Yupik

The Siberian Yupik Eskimos,[3] one of the groups of indigenous people of the Chukchi Peninsula, live predominantly in communities along the peninsula's southern Bering Sea coast in Russia and on St. Lawrence Island in Alaska (Figure 1). The word "Eskimo," which is tied to the language of the Indian tribes of Abenaki and Athabaskans, means "raw-eaters"—that is, "those who eat raw meat." During the eighteenth and nineteenth centuries, the term became firmly established in the literature of the American north, after which it began to appear as a self-designation among the Eskimo population itself. Sometime after that, the far north peoples of Asia also began to refer to themselves as "Eskimos." Today, the term has been rejected by

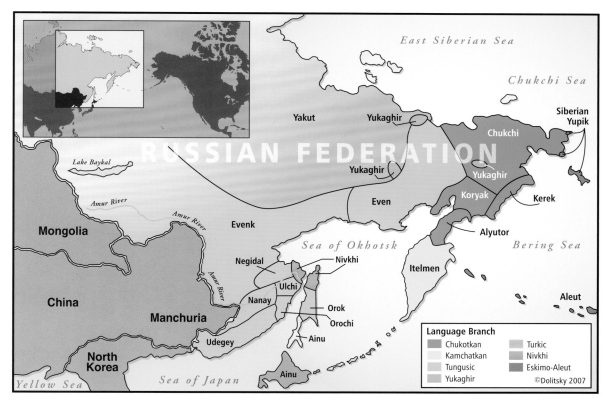

Figure 1. Populations and Speakers of the Asian North Pacific Region Languages.

---

3 *Yupik*, meaning "real person"; *Yupigyt*, "real people"—both derived from *yuk*, "person."

most in favor of the original self-designation *Yupik*, but is used herein to harmonize the text with the Russian language versions of the tales, which were translated from recordings of the stories made in the early twentieth century.

Once numerous, the Siberian Yupik declined in population during the eighteenth and nineteenth centuries due to infectious diseases and frequent conflicts with their neighbors. Presently, they number about 4,500 - 5,000, of whom 2,000 live in Russia.[4] There are about 80,000 Eskimos worldwide. In genetic affinity, Siberian Yupik are tied to the North American and Greenlandic Eskimos. The Eskimo language is spoken in 25 dialects and has distant affinity with the Aleut language. Until the twentieth century, the Siberian Yupik Eskimos were divided into three groups: Chaplino, Sireniki, and Naukan.[5]

Alexander Dolitsky with the residents of the Chukchi-Eskimo village, Lorino.
July, 2006. Courtesy of Alexander Dolitsky.

4 Национальная Принадлежность и Владение Русским Языком. (National Identity and Knowledge of the Russian Langauge). Всероссийская перепись населения 2002 года. Федеральная служба государственной статистики, 2004 www.gks./ru/perepis/t5.htm.

5 William Fitzhugh, "Eskimos: Hunters of the Frozen Coasts," *Crossroads of the Continents: Cultures of Siberia and Alaska*. William Fitzhugh and Aron Crowell (eds). Washington, D.C.: The Smithsonian Institution Press, 1988, pp. 45-6.

From earliest times, the Siberian Yupik Eskimos maintained close and continuous cultural and economic contact with the aboriginal peoples of the Chukchi and Kamchatka Peninsulas and western Alaska. Since Siberian Yupik Eskimos also were in close contact with the people of St. Lawrence Island and western Alaska, they often served as intermediaries in the trade between Chukchi and Alaskan Eskimos.[6] The economy of the Siberian Yupik, similar to that of the Alaskan Yupik, centered around sea-mammal hunting, supplemented by fishing and terrestrial hunting and gathering. This subsistence maritime emphasis is reflected in their oral traditions.

Interaction between the Siberian Yupik Eskimos and their Chukotka, Kamchatka, and Alaska neighbors is evident in commonalities found in the genres and subjects of their oral narratives. In fact, the origins of the tales of the Chukchi and Siberian Yupik are difficult to assign with certainty to one group or the other. Due to centuries of intercultural contact among the coastal dwellers resulting from the reindeer-herding patterns of the Chukchi and also due to shared ecological and social conditions, the majority of the tales recorded among the Chukchi parallel or share many elements with the folklore of the Siberian Yupik Eskimos.

In the mid-twentieth century, as part of Soviet state building and collectivization, the economies of the coast dwellers and the inland reindeer herders became unified, with the state-sponsored formation of composite hunting-herding cooperatives (*kolkhozy*), in which the Eskimo and Chukchi populations were made to coexist. Up to that time, Siberian Yupik Eskimos had lived in large semi-sedentary clan-based villages along the coast in round semi-subterranean structures (*yarangas* or *zemlyankas*[7]) occupied by communal families of given clans.[8] In the 1950s, many of these Eskimo villages were consolidated or relocated by the Soviet government according to the central government's economic plans. Today, the Siberian Yupik live in well-equipped houses and make use of many modern amenities.

Writing was first introduced to the Yupik Eskimos of Siberia in 1932. With the organization of a mixed traditional Chukchi-Siberian Yupik and planned Soviet economy, consolidation of villages, and the acquisition of the Russian language, the indigenous languages of the Russian Far East have fallen out of common use.

---

6 William Fitzhugh, "Eskimos: Hunters of the Frozen Coasts," *Crossroads of the Continents: Cultures of Siberia and Alaska*. William Fitzhugh and Aron Crowell (eds). Washington, D.C.: The Smithsonian Institution Press, 1988, pp. 45-6.

7 *Zemlyanka* (Russian)—The semi-subterranean wooden dwellings of Eskimos, Coastal Chukchi, and Koryaks. The dwellings were made of driftwood, whale bones, turf, and/or stone.

8 William Fitzhugh, "Eskimos: Hunters of the Frozen Coasts," *Crossroads of the Continents: Cultures of Siberia and Alaska*. William Fitzhugh and Aron Crowell (eds). Washington, D.C.: The Smithsonian Institution Press, 1988, pp. 45-6.

The ethnographer W.G. Bogoras first recorded the folklore of the Siberian Yupik Eskimos in 1901. During the Soviet period (1917-1991), many additional narratives, including those found herein, were collected and published by Eskimo language and culture specialists.

Chukchi

The Chukchi, who call themselves *Lugora Vetlat*, that is "the true people" or "the real people," are another of the indigenous groups of the Chukchi Peninsula (Figure 1). The term "Chukchi" was derived from the Chukchi ethnonym *chauchu*—the self-designation of the nomadizing Chukchi reindeer herders. The coastal Chukchi originally called themselves *ankalyu*, meaning "at the sea" or "coast-dwellers" (derived from *anke*, meaning "sea"). Adopted as early as the seventeenth century by the first Russian explorers, the term "Chukchi" soon found its place in the literature and later began to be used by the Chukchi as a self-designating term.

The Chukchi, as distinguishable from the coastal maritime tribes of the Kamchatka Peninsula and Okhotsk seacoast, were formed as a result of the northward movement of hunters and reindeer herders at the beginning of the second millennium A.D. During this period, the present-day Koryaks and Itelmens also were formed. The Chukchi neighbors of the Bering Sea coast include the Siberian Yupik and Alaskan Eskimo; to the southeast the Koryak and Kerek; and to the northwest the Even, Yakut, and Yukagir (Figure 1). As a result of these peoples' geographical proximity, a significant number of Maritime Chukchi descended genetically from their seacoast neighbors. Reindeer hunters, the ancestors of the Chukchi and Koryak, probably occupied the interior regions of Chukotka for at least 3,000 years.[9] Archaeological and ethnographic evidence suggests that the Chukchi and Koryak reindeer-herding groups make up a homogeneous ethno-linguistic population with similar, mutually understandable languages, names, and material and spiritual cultures. Despite apparent differences between Reindeer and Maritime Chukchi, they share similarities as well, due to their common dependence on the subsistence resources of northern northeast Asia.

---

9 Sergey Arutyunov, "Chukchi: Warriors and Traders of Chukotka," *Crossroads of the Continents: Cultures of Siberia and Alaska*. William Fitzhugh and Aron Crowell (eds). Washington, D.C.: The Smithsonian Institution Press, 1988, p. 39.

Residents of the Chukchi village, Inchoun. July, 2008. Photo by Alexander Dolitsky.

The Chukchi numbered about 16,000 in 2002.[10] They settled in the Chukchi national *okrug* (rural district) and, in part, in the Koryak national *okrug* and in the Sakha Republic, the former Yakutsk Autonomous Soviet Socialist Republic (Figure 1).

The traditional occupations of the Chukchi included nomadic reindeer herding, hunting of sea mammals and fur-bearers, and fishing. Breeding animals in captivity emerged fairly recently as an economic activity. In the early 1950s, the economies of both settled and nomadic Chukchi were consolidated in reindeer herding-hunting cooperatives (*kolkhozy*). A number of hunting and reindeer-herding state-run cooperatives (*sovkhozy*) were organized in the *okrug* in the 1960s and at the beginning of the 1970s. In the 1990s, as a result of economic and political reforms in Russia, the Chukchi national *okrug* seceded from the Magadan *oblast* (administrative district) and received economic and political autonomy within Russia.

With the development of a written alphabet in the early twentieth century, the Chukchi language began to be written down, leading to a rapid increase in literacy

---

10 Национальная Принадлежность и Владение Русским Языком. [National Identity and Knowledge of the Russian Langauge]. Всероссийская перепись населения 2002 года. Федеральная служба государственной статистики, 2004 www.gks./ru/perepis/t5.htm.

and consequent social changes. A newspaper was published in the Chukchi language, as well as other literature. By 1931, the Kamchatkan area, which at the time included the present territories of Kamchatka and Chukotka, had become home to 123 schools, including 62 boarding schools that housed 3,000 Native students—20 percent of all Native children of school age in the Russian Far North. Today, the Chukchi have their own indigenous teachers, writers, doctors, scientists, artists, livestock specialists, and other professionals.

Up to the end of the 1950s, the Chukchi lived in traditional semi-subterranean dwellings covered with walrus and reindeer pelts. Chukchi communities now boast up-to-date dwellings and social service buildings. Electricity, radio, public baths, hospitals, schools, boarding schools, cultural centers, stores, and centralized heating systems all occupy a place in the contemporary life of the Chukchi.

Bogoras first undertook scientific research of Chukchi folklore in the 1890s. Later, during the Soviet period (1917 to 1991), specialists in the Chukchi language carried out the extensive recording of Chukchi tales and legends.

HOW SWAN FOUND HAPPINESS

This happened long, long ago, when people lived off the gifts of the land and sea, when winter did not quarrel with summer, and when majestic glaciers proudly stood in the mountain valleys. In those faraway times, Raven reigned as master of the sky; Wolf prowled deep into the tangled forest; Beaver swam unbothered in the secluded pond; and Fox hunted freely alongside the flowing brook. All of these creatures lived where they should be living, where their ancestors, after living there many long years, had left them a memorable legacy. They were at home.

Only white Swan was a stranger in this faraway land, struggling to find his natural place. A ferocious wind had blown up from the sea and swept him away from his native flock, carrying him far inland into this strange land. When he tried to rest in a forest meadow, Raven would screech down at him and Wolf would chase after him. If he landed in the middle of the pond, Beaver would threaten him and chase him off, too. When he landed on the river, Fox, fussing about on the bank, would rush toward him, defending her burrow from the foreign white bird.

So it was that Swan found himself hurrying from one place to another in search of a welcoming, compassionate, cozy home—in search of happiness.

Owl, noticing the lone Swan flying about unable to find his place, spoke to him. "Listen, Swan, you will never find peace on this land that is so strange and foreign to you. You will never find love and happiness here. You should fly away to another place."

Ruffling his feathers, Swan replied, "And where would I fly to? A wind from the sea carried me here against my will. It took me away from my native flock. Time will pass," he assured Owl, "and my forest neighbors will become friendly. One day, they will accept me into their world."

Owl listened attentively, turned his head to the right, then to the left, peered at Swan with huge round eyes, blinked, and said, "Come see me in the spring, when the salmonberries begin to ripen and the red salmon are just about to swim up the river to spawn. If by spring you have found happiness, a new home, and love in this land, I'll give you my respect. If not, I'll give you my advice."

Swan flew away into the cold winter. For months he hid in the forest out of sight of the animals, away from their homes. When spring arrived, he flew back to where he had met Owl and confessed to him, "I'm so tired. I haven't been able to find happiness, a new home, and the love of others in this land. Tell me what to do! Where should I go? Where should I live?"

Owl pondered for a moment and replied, "To find the happiness you seek, you must overcome your fears. You will be tested three times. Each time you must defeat evil and cowardice with kindness and bravery. Here is my feather. Fly wherever it flies and stop wherever it stops."

The feather took flight, sailing off toward the setting sun, Swan flying along behind it. How long they flew, who can say? They flew across seven forests. The feather flew ahead, finally alighting in a forest meadow. Landing behind it, Swan caught sight of Wolf sitting still in the meadow. His leg was caught in a trap! Seeing Swan approaching, Wolf growled softly at him, then yelped in pain. Having no choice, Wolf begged Swan to help him get free from the trap. Swan pricked up his ears, thinking: "He chased me out of the forest. He wanted to rip me to pieces, to shred me. How can I trust him? I will only make myself easy prey for him! But, if I help him, maybe we will become friends, and he will share with me his forest home." Swan wanted to trust Wolf, but he was afraid. Wolf yelped in pain again. He looked at Swan, his eyes filled with desperation. "I must help him, even if he might try to tear me to shreds," decided Swan.

Swan approached the howling Wolf. Using all of his strength, he pressed his beak between the trap's jagged jaws and pried with all of his might, until at last the trap sprung open, freeing Wolf's leg. Wolf stood up on all fours and limped away. At the forest's edge, he turned and smiled his thanks to Swan.

Owl's feather took to the sky again, and Swan followed. They flew across seven lakes. The feather, light as a faded autumn leaf, softly descended onto a lonely, sleepy lake. And so did Swan. Swan's heart began pounding when he heard Beaver's tail slapping the water nearby. "Oh, Beaver will attack me and kill me," frightened Swan whispered to himself, as he paddled quietly to the edge of the lake to hide in the tall grass.

Beaver was building a dam. But spring thaw had brought a flood. No matter how many sticks and branches Beaver put in place, he could not stop the water that poured out of the lake and into the stream. Swan watched as Beaver swam back and forth with branches, crawling along more and more slowly with each trip as he ran out of energy; he could not do it by himself. Swan knew if Beaver did not get his dam built, he would never survive the cold winter.

So Swan said to Beaver, "I can help you build the dam. I can bring you many twigs and branches, and together we will stop up this stream. And for my help, maybe you'll allow me to live on this lake."

In response, Beaver turned his back and set off to weave some branches into the dam. "Well," contemplated Beaver to himself, "I can't do this by myself. I need help. The lake is big enough for two." Turning back to Swan, Beaver indignantly muttered, "Fine, help me. And you can live here, too. But only at the other end of the lake." Beaver then sank into the water and continued his work.

Swan brought many twigs and branches. Working together, Beaver and Swan built a dam so strong no flowing stream could penetrate it. Swan watched as Beaver used his last ounce of energy to dive down and crawl into the safety of his dam.

The feather flitted off over Swan's head, again floating in the direction of the sunset. Swan took flight behind it. They flew across seven rivers. The feather landed on the bank of a tumbling brook, with Swan landing beside it, not far from Fox's den. Spotting Swan, Fox, fearing for her kits, began to fuss. She tried to fool Swan, walking slowly away in hopes of enticing the white bird away from the den.

"Don't be afraid of me," pleaded Swan. "I have landed here in search of happiness, and not to get your kits. I'll be a kind and true neighbor; I'll protect your den."

Swan turned to Fox for an answer, but Fox squinted her eyes and looked back at Swan in puzzlement. "Protect us?" she wondered. "That strange white bird could be trying to trick me. But, then, he does seem to be sincere."

"I'll warn you of danger from the sky and bravely defend your home and your kits," continued Swan.

"Swan would be able to see everything from up in the sky," considered Fox. "Indeed, he could be a very helpful neighbor and is too proud and trustworthy for deceit."

"All right, I'll share this place with you, but right now I need to go hunting," she said, running off into the woods.

"What's that?" Swan puzzled. Suddenly he found himself standing right at the very place Owl's feather had first flown from in search of happiness. All around him, on the lakes and ponds, water lilies burned fire red, birds sang… And directly in front of him stood a female Swan of unusual beauty. He had never seen such a graceful swan in all his life. Behind the female Swan sat Owl, looking at him with frank admiration.

"In following the feather, you feared nothing; you listened to your heart, not your fears," said Owl. "You withstood all tests and challenges. You defeated evil with good deeds. By offering help, you gained friendship; and by your courage, you acquired freedom. Thus you have found happiness, love, and your home."

The two swans thanked Owl for his wisdom and good words. They spread their wings wide, and together flew into the unbounded blue sky, over the forests, lakes, and rivers—their new place.

So the two swans became mates. They loved each other and lived happily in their new home for many, many years.

The end.

Как лебедь счастье нашёл

то было давно, это ещё тогда было, когда люди жили от даров земли и моря, когда зима не спорила с летом, когда величавые ледники гордо стояли в долинах гор. В те далёкие времена Ворон был хозяином неба, Волк бродил в непроходимых лесах, Бобёр плавал в уединённых прудах и Лиса охотилась у журчащих рек. Все жили там, где должны были жить, где их предки жили долгие годы, оставив памятное о себе наследие. Они жили в родном краю.

Только белый Лебедь был чужестранцем в этих краях, не мог найти родное местечко. Свирепый заморский ветер унёс его от родной стаи и забросил в чуждую ему землю. Так и жил он один на этой земле. Прилетит на лесную поляну — на него Ворон накричит, Волк завоет — прогоняют его. На пруд прилетит — ему Бобёр грозит, из пруда гонит. На реку сядет — Лиса с недоверием суетится у берега, нору защищает от странной белой птицы, боится Лебедя.

Так и метался Лебедь из одного места в другое в поисках уютного, приветливого, дружелюбного дома — в поисках счастья.

Видит Сова, что одинокий Лебедь мечется, не может себя найти и говорит ему:

«Послушай Лебедь, не будет тебе покоя на этой чуждой для тебя земле, не найдёшь ты себе здесь счастья и любви. Улетай-ка ты в другие края».

А гордый Лебедь встрепехнул своими перьями и отвечает:

«Да куда уж мне лететь? Занёс меня сюда заморский ветер не по моей воле, оторвал от моей родной стаи. Вот пройдёт время и мои лесные соседи подобрее станут и примут меня в свой мир».

Сова слушала внимательно, повернула голову направо, потом налево, взглянула на Лебедя своими большущими круглыми глазами, моргнула и сказала:

«Приходи ко мне этой весной, когда морошка цвести начнёт и нерка в реки зайдёт на нерест. Если к тому времени найдёшь на этой земле счастье, мир и любовь — моё почтение тебе, а если нет — то совет тебе дам».

Улетел Лебедь в холодную зиму и прятался от всех, где мог. А как пришла весна, он вернулся к Сове и признался:

«Намаялся я, не могу найти счастье, мир и любовь в этих краях. Скажи, что делать? Куда идти? Где жить?»

Сова призадумалась на мгновение и ответила:

«Чтобы найти счастье, которое ты ищешь, ты должен пройти через три испытания, преодолеть три страха, —где добро и храбрость победит зло и трусость. Вот тебе моё перо: лети туда, куда оно полетит, остановись там, где оно остановится».

Полетело перо на закат — Лебедь за ним. Долго-ли летели, кто знает? Через семь лесов перелетели. Летит перо впереди, село на лесной поляне, а за ним Лебедь. Видит, сидит на поляне Волк — капканом ему лапу зажало. Увидел Волк Лебедя и взвыл, просит помочь ему из капкана освободиться. Лебедь насторожился и думает: «Он меня из леса выгонял, загрызть хотел, разорвать на клочья. Как же ему верить? Как бы самому добычей не стать? Но если доброе дело сделаю и помогу ему из беды выбраться, тогда мы друзьями станем, его лес и моим лесом станет. Ну да ладно, помогу ему».

Так подумал Лебедь, подлетел к изморённому Волку, напрягся из всех своих сил и клювом вытащил зажатую в капкан лапу. Волк встал на все четыре лапы и хромая убежал в лес с благодарностью в глазах.

Снова взлетело совиное перо в небо и Лебедь за ним. Через семь озёр перелетели. Как увядший осенний листок перо мягко опустилось на водную гладь спящего, одинокого озера и Лебедь туда же. Увидел Лебедь Бобра, забилось у него сердце: «Ой, нападёт на меня Бобёр, убьёт меня», —с испугом подумал Лебедь.

Tamara 2011

А Бобёр дамбу строит, но никак не может вытекающий из озера ручей перекрыть — весенняя оттепель много воды в реки и озёра принесла. Совсем из сил выбился, не по плечу это одному. Не построит добротную дамбу до осенних дождей, тогда зимой ему худо будет. Не выжить Бобру холодную зиму без дамбы.

Лебедь говорит Бобру:

«Я помогу тебе дамбу построить, принесу много хвороста и вместе мы ручей этот быстро перекроем. А за мою помощь, ты мне позволь на этом озере жить».

А Бобёр давай дальше сучья перекладывать, из тунеля выбираться — совсем измучился. «Ну да ладно, —размышляет Бобёр, —самому мне не справиться, помощь нужна. А озеро большое, на двоих хватит».

«Ладно, помоги, и тогда жить здесь будешь, только в том конце озера», —с негодованием буркнул Бобёр и ушёл под воду.

Притащил Лебедь много сучьев и вдвоём они быстро построили добротную дамбу, перекрыли ручей.

И перо снова запорхало на закат, а за ним Лебедь. Перелетели через семь рек. Село перо на берегу бурлящей реки и Лебедь там же сел, недалеко от лисьей норы. Увидела Лиса Лебедя, засуетилась, за своих лисят боится, всё пытается обхитрить Лебедя, от норы его увести.

«Не бойся меня, —сказал Лебедь. —За счастьем я сюда прилетел, а не за твоими лисятами. Я буду добрым и верным соседом, ещё в небе буду тебя об опасности предупреждать, буду храбро защищать твой дом, твоих лисят».

Прищурилась Лиса и думает: «А действительно, он полезным соседом будет, хитрить не умеет, уж слишком горд и полон достоинства». Так согласилась Лиса жить с Лебедем на одной реке, и ушла охотиться в лес.

«Что такое?» —удивился Лебедь. Вдруг видит, что он оказался на том же месте, где Сова сидела, откуда перо полетело за счастьем. А вокруг, на озёрах и прудах, лилии красным пламенем горят, птицы щебечут… И прямо перед ним стоит Лебёдушка необыкновенной красоты! Такую грациозную Лебёдушку он ещё никогда не видел. А за ней Сова сидит.

Посмотрела Сова на Лебедя с одобрением и говорит:

«Не побоялся ты трудностей, следовал за моим пером и преодолел все испытания и страхи. Добром ты победил зло, помощью ты завоевал дружбу, храбростью ты приобрёл свободу — поэтому и нашёл своё счастье, свою любовь и родной дом».

Tomada 2011

Поблагодарили Лебедь с Лебёдушкой Сову за мудрость и добрые слова, широко расправили крылья и полетели вместе в необъятное голубое небо над лесами, озёрами и реками — над новым краем.

Так два Лебедя стали парой, любили друг друга и жили счастливо в родном краю долгие, долгие годы.

Конец.

THE QUARREL BETWEEN SUN AND MOON

o it was. One time Sun and Moon got into a quarrel about who was more important and who should be the master of Earth.

Said Sun to Moon: "When I rise, every living thing on Earth rises with me—the people, animals, forests, and fields. I bring them warmth and light. Every living thing originates from me and every living creature depends on me. Without me, there would be no life."

Moon replied, "And when you disappear beyond the horizon, I come to replace you. I bring quiet and comfort to all. The oceans and seas are attracted to me with their incoming and outgoing tides. I reveal the stars in the heavens. At night, I become a beacon for all living creatures, a compass for people and animals. Without me, there would be no life."

Sun and Moon argued endlessly on and on, neither able to convince the other who was more important and who deserved to rule Earth. They were so stubborn, they could hear only their own voices; neither could hear the other's reasons.

Finally, growing tired of arguing, they agreed to ask Day and Night to decide which of them was more important.

17

"Day—tell us. Which of us is more important? Who has the right to be the master of Earth? Sun or Moon? You decide!"

Lit up in bright, iridescent colors, Day, drawing from his own brilliant insight, pondered the questions and replied, "From sunrise to sunset, I see Sun; I encounter only him. He brings light, warmth, joy, and energy to all. Yes, yes, sometimes he does also bring misfortune—drought, harsh heat, fires . . . But without Sun, I would not have a place on Earth! Yes, Sun is more important. Sun should be the master of Earth!"

Sun smiled at Day with gratitude, glowing yet brighter from a thrilling pride. "Yes, I am more important," he muttered to himself giddily.

Sun and Moon then turned to Night.

"Night—tell us. Which of us is more important? Who has the right to be the master of Earth? You be the judge!"

Night grew dark, then even darker—pitch dark, falling quiet as an evening mist. Then said Night in a soft voice, "From sunset to dawn, I see only Moon. I live alone with Moon and all of the stars. Moon brings serenity, rest, and mystery, and, after sunset, she lights the Earth. Yes, sometimes her tides are too high. And sometimes she disappears, leaving the world in darkness . . ."

Night's voice was so quiet and calm, Sun, Moon, and Day had to lean in to hear it. "But without Moon," continued Night, "I could not exist! She is my partner and my neighbor. Moon is worthier. Moon should rule Earth!"

Shining bright and full, Moon glanced at Night gratefully; and with a newfound confidence Moon whispered under her breath, "Yes, sometimes a whisper speaks louder than a shout. All in all, I am more important!"

Thus Sun and Moon failed to resolve their argument. They did not know whom to ask or where else to turn for advice.

Hovering silently nearby, Wind, hearing the quarrel of Sun and Moon, grew exasperated by their pride and arrogance. Suddenly blowing in from all directions, Wind addressed Sun and Moon in a loud voice, "I exist in all regions. I travel everywhere. I gather clouds that neither of you can penetrate, devastating Earth at will with hurricanes, storms, and tornadoes. When I come with my frost, I freeze the entire land. I cover the rivers and lakes with ice. And when I arrive with snow, I cover all of the land with it. I hide everything under the snow. But I also bring cool, drying breezes and caress all living creatures.

"I watch over you from all remote corners of Earth during both day and night. I scatter clouds to reveal your beauty and power. If not for me, you would remain hidden behind the clouds forever. Indeed, without any one of the three of us, there would be no life on Earth.

"Who of you is more important, you ask? I'll tell you." Wind resumed, "To me, everything is equal and everyone is important. But it is the one who lives in peace, the one who appreciates others and treats them with kindness, and who endeavors to make life better for everyone—that one is worthiest!"

Embarrassed, Sun and Moon lowered their heads. Memories of their long debate now filled them with shame. "So, how should we settle our argument? How can we once again find peace between us? Doesn't someone have to be the master of Earth?" they asked Wind sheepishly.

Wind stepped back and drew a deep breath. Puffing up his powerful cheeks, his huge round eyes of an ox wide and bulging, he looked at Sun and Moon with a penetrating stare.

"You agree between yourselves," he spoke. "Day is for Sun. And Night is for Moon."

Sun and Moon lowered their eyes; they stood silent and still.

"You are both important and worthy," continued Wind. "Each of you is the master of your own realm. Live in this world in peace—for yourselves and for others!"

And that's all.

День засиял радужными цветами, призадумался на мгновение и ответил:

«От восхода до заката я только Солнце вижу, только с ним встречаюсь. Оно приносит всем тепло, энергию и радость. Да, но иногда оно приносит и беду — засуху, зной и пожары... Но без Солнца и мне места на Земле нет! Солнце важнее, для меня Солнце хозяин!»

Улыбнулось Солнце Дню с благодарностью, понравился ему ответ. Ещё ярче засияло от трепещущей гордости и счастливо прошептало:

«Да, я важнее, я хозяин Земли».

А потом обратились Солнце и Луна к Ночи:

«Ночь, скажи нам, кто из нас важнее? Кто хозян Земли? Будь нашим судьёй!»

Ночь ещё больше потемнела, затихла на мгновение и ответила тихим голосом:

«От заката до восхода я только Луну вижу, только с ней встречаюсь. Она приносит покой, отдых, таинство и свет в ночи. Да, иногда её приливы очень высокие. И иногда она исчезает, оставляя всех в холоде и в кромешной тьме...»

Солнце, Луна и День наклонились ближе к Ночи, чтобы услышать её мягкий голос.

«Но без Луны, —продолжала Ночь, —и мне не быть! Она мой партнёр и мой сосед. Луна важнее, Луна — хозяин!»

Засияла Луна на звёздном небе, улыбнулась Ночи и с уверенностью подумала: «И всё-таки я важнее, быть мне хозяином Земли!»

Так и не решили Солнце и Луна свой спор — не знают кого-же ещё спросить, к кому за советом обратиться.

И вот блуждающий вблизи Ветер услышал этот спор, возмутился самолюбием и эгоизмом Солнца и Луны, задул во все стороны и гневным голосом сказал:

«Во всех краях я бываю. Облака, через которые ни одному из вас не проникнуть собираю; штормы, смерчи и ураганы приношу всему живому; разрушаю города и селения. А когда с холодом приду, всю землю заморожу. Реки и озёра льдом скую, всю землю снегом занесу, всё под снегом спрячу. Но также свежесть и ласку даю всем на Земле».

«Я днём и ночью за вами слежу, со всех уголков мира за вами наблюдаю. А разогнав облака, я всем на свете показываю вашу красоту и величие; без меня вы навсегда бы остались в кромешной тьме... Это без нас троих не быть жизни на Земле!»

«Вы спрашиваете, кто из вас важнее? Я отвечу, —продолжал Ветер. —Для меня, все на свете равны и все важны. А сильнее и важнее тот, кто в добре с другими живёт и добро им приносит!»

Засмущались Солнце и Луна, опустили свои головы, стыдно им стало за своё самолюбие и эгоизм, и спросили они у Ветра робким голосом:

«Так как же наш спор решить? Как нам снова в мире жить? Ведь должен быть кто-то хозяином Земли!»

Ветер глубоко вздохнул, надул свои могучие щёки, вытаращил большущие круглые глаза, посмотрел на обоих проницательным взглядом и молвил:

«А вы между собой договоритесь, что Солнце — Днём, Луна — Ночью. Вы оба важны, вы оба хозяева своих владений. И живите вы в мире для себя и для других!»

Вот и всё.

THE TWO STRONGMEN AND THE OLDSTER

n the island of Kigi, there lived a man who had been suckled by a wolf. They called him Ettuvi. And, in Yanrakinot, there lived another man who had been suckled by a brown bear. They called him Kaynuvi. From the milk of their animals they had derived enormous strength. They had never seen each other, but Ettuvi from Kigi had heard that Kaynuvi was very strong; and the people of Yanrakinot told Kaynuvi that there was nobody stronger in the world than Ettuvi. Through his people, each sent word to the other of his desire to compare their strengths in a great contest.

One day an old man from Yanrakinot was casting a fishing net into the lagoon. In the bottom of his *baydara*, his open skin boat, lay two hard *poplavoks*—seal-skin floats. Suddenly, he caught sight of the two strongmen—Ettuvi and Kaynuvi—coming toward him. "Watch us, old man," they said, "as we compete in our strength. And tell us who is stronger!"

The old man replied, "Wait for me here while I place the net."

Keeping his eyes on the strongmen, the old man spread the net slowly. While he worked, Ettuvi and Kaynuvi lay down on the sand, propped up their chins with their hands and talked peacefully to each other. From the sand, Kaynuvi picked up a bone

from the joint of a walrus flipper and crumbled it into dust with his fingers. Ettuvi's elbows rested on a float made of seal skin. He reached to pick it up to mend it, and had barely touched it when the float collapsed.

The little old man watched all of this out of the corner of his eye as he continued to work. When his net was spread, he said to them, "You have already competed. One of you has turned a bone into dust with his fingers, and the other, by just a light touch of his hand, has collapsed a float made of seal skin.

"Could you not, Ettuvi, say that your body is better at making dust of bones? And you, Kaynuvi, could you not say that your body is better at squashing floats of seal skin filled with air?

"Both of you are so strong that if you start competing you will kill each other. It will be better if you don't fight! And, you know, you live in different villages!"

The strongmen listened to the old man from Yanrakinot. They did not fight. Each went his own way.

That is all. And that's the way I heard it.

Два силача и старик

ил на острове Киги человек, волком вскормленный. Звали его Эттувьи. А в Янракиноте жил другой человек, вскормленный бурым медведем, его звали Кайнувьи. От животного молока силу они огромную получили. Оба друг друга никогда не видели. Но кигмитский Эттувьи слышал, что Кайнувьи очень силён, а Кайнувьи люди говорили, что сильнее Эттувьи никого на свете нет.

Передали они через людей друг другу весть, что хотят помериться силой. Вот однажды янракинотский старичок поставил в лагуне рыбаловные сети. На его байдаре было два тугих поплавка из пёстрой нерпы. Вдруг видит, идут два силача — Эттувьи и Кайнувьи. Подошли они к старичку и сказали:

«Смотри, старик, как мы будем в силе состязаться, да скажи потом, кто из нас сильнее».

Старичок ответил:

«Подождите меня здесь, пока я сеть поставлю».

Распровляет сеть не спеша, а сам глаз с силачей не спускает. Легли силачи на песок и подпёрли подбородки, разговаривают мирно друг с другом. Оказалась под рукой у Кайнувьи кость от сустава моржового ласта. Взял он эту кость

и раскрошил её пальцами в порошок. А Эттувьи облокотился на поплавок из нерпичьей шкуры, хотел его поправить. Только задел рукой, поплавок не выдержал и лопнул. Старичок всё это видел. Расправил он сети и сказал им:

«Вот вы и посостязались: один пальцами кость раскрошил, другой одним приксоновением раздавил поплавок из нерпичьей шкуры. А ты, Эттувьи, разве можешь сказать, что тело твоё крепче раздавленной кости? А ты, Кайнувьи, разве скажешь, что тело твоё крепче поплавка из надутой нерпичьей шкуры? Оба вы такие силачи, что начнёте состязаться и убьёте друг друга. Лучше уж не боритесь! Ведь вы в разных селениях живёте!»

Послушались янракинотского старичка силачи и не стали бороться, разошлись.

Всё. Слышал я это в таком виде.

THE RAVEN
AND THE OWL

n long ago times, there lived together in one dwelling a raven and an owl. The two coexisted in a friendly manner. They didn't quarrel and always shared their catch. The raven and the owl were both female. And both were white.

They lived on like that as a happy pair, until the time came that they began to worry. One day, the owl said to the raven, "We'll get old, we'll die, our children and grandchildren will resemble us: they'll be the same as we are—white."

Then the owl asked the raven to paint her, to make her beautiful. The raven agreed. She took the old blubber oil from a *zhirnik*, a stone oil lamp, poured it into a pot, and with a feather from her tail began carefully to make marks on the owl. The owl sat still, not stirring. The raven painted the owl all day. When the raven was finished, she said to the owl, "As soon as you dry out, paint me!"

The owl agreed. Once her feathers had dried, she said to the raven, "Now I will paint you. Close your eyes and sit there. Don't get up!"

The raven sat there with her eyes closed, not allowing herself to stir. Setting the brush aside, the owl lifted the pot and poured all of the oil over the raven, turning her completely black. When the raven realized what had happened, she became very angry.

"Eh, how badly you've treated me!" cried the raven. "I painted you with such care. I wasn't lazy. Look how beautiful you've become! From now on there'll be no love lost between us! And our grandchildren and great-grandchildren will be enemies. The ravens will never forgive you for this. Look how black you've made me! How conspicuous! Now we'll be outright strangers! Enemies forever!"

And so it has been that, since that day, raven's feathers have been black and owl's feathers have been mottled.

The end of the tale.

Ворониха и совиха

В давнее время жили вдвоём в одном жилище ворониха и совиха.

Дружно жили, не ссорились, добычу всегда вместе ели. А были эти ворониха с совихой — женщины. И ещё были они обе совсем белые.

Так они жили вдвоём и вот стали стариться. Сказала совиха воронихе:

«Состаримся мы, умрём, будут наши дети и внуки на нас похожи: такие же, как мы, белые».

И попросила совихаervорониху, чтобы раскрасила она её, красивой сделала. Согласилась ворониха. Взяла старый жир из светильника-жирника, вылила его в котелок и пером из своего хвоста начала раскрашивать. Сидит совиха, замерла, не шелохнётся. Весь день ворониха совиху раскрашивала. Кончила раскрашивать, сказала:

«Как только высохнешь, и меня покрась!»

Согласилась совиха. Высохли у неё перья, она и говорит воронихе:

«Теперь я тебя раскрашивать буду. Зажмурься и сиди, не двигайся!»

Сидит ворониха, зажмурилась, шелохнуться не смеет. А совиха взяла жир из котелка, да на ворониху весь и вылила, всю очернила. Рассердилась ворониха, обиделась на совиху.

«Эх, как ты плохо поступила! —закричала ворониха. —Я тебя так старательно раскрасила, не ленилась. Смотри, какая ты красивая получилась! Навсегда теперь между нами вражда ляжет! И внуки и правнуки наши враждовать будут. Никогда вороны тебе не простят этого. Видишь, какой чёрной ты меня сделала, какой приметной. Мы теперь с тобой совсем чужие будем, враги навсегда!»

Вот с тех пор все вороны чёрные, а все совы пёстрые.

Конец сказке.

THE MOUSE AND THE MOUNTAIN

hey say it was like this. At one time, there was no mountain at the end of the Chaplino spit, beyond the lake. Then, all of a sudden, it appeared. The people call the mountain Afsynakhak, which means Mouse. And they say this is how it came to be.

Once, a pensive little mouse asked himself: "Why is it that for people there are flattering tales and songs, but for our breed of mice you don't hear anything good? People become heroes, wizards, brave hunters, runners, and jumpers. But mice, never! We become nothing! What could I do to make my kin famous among people? Well, what I'll do is to gnaw through this huge tree, throw it on my back, and carry it to the top of the mountain. At last, people will see that there is a mouse superhero, a strongmouse!"

And so the mouse began to gnaw through the tree, stopping on occasion to rock it from side to side. But the tree would not fall. He then started to gnaw fiercely. The tree rocked slightly and finally fell. The mouse rejoiced in his success—until he noticed that he had not cut down a tree, but a high blade of grass. Feeling quite embarrassed by his blunder, he thought: "Good thing the neighbors didn't see this—how they would have laughed! But what can I do so that the entire world will know my strength?"

The mouse scampered off across the tundra until he found himself before a very large lake. "I'll swim across this lake," he thought. "Then I'll sit down on the other shore and I'll dry out my *kukhlyanka*-fur coat, breeches, and *torbaza*-boots. People will see me and say, 'What a swimmer! What a big lake he swam across!' They will tell tales about me! They will sing songs!"

The mouse jumped in and began to swim across the lake. Halfway across, he became so tired he almost drowned. After barely making it to the opposite shore, he spread out his clothes to dry. He was sitting on a pebble when he saw a man coming. As the man walked by, he left footprints in the wet ground, and in each footprint a large lake appeared. "Oh, now I see how large a lake I swam across," thought the mouse. It hurt him to realize how little he was!

The mouse put on his still-damp clothes and started off toward a rounded mountain that stood up ahead. Stopping in front of the mountain, he thought back on his failures and became so upset that he had to stop himself from crying. Gathering his strength, the mouse ran to the mountain, hoisted it onto his back in a fit of temper, and carried it to the north side. He carried it and carried it until he got so tired he had to stop to rest. He could see the village Tyflyak up ahead. The mouse thought: "I'll go to Tyflyak and take a little rest. People will see me and they'll say, 'Oho, what a superhero! What a strongmouse! He brought a mountain!' They will tell tales about me and sing songs about me!" He shifted the mountain on his back so that he could carry it better. From the shaking, a pebble fell off the mountain, rolled down, and struck the mouse on the head. The mouse squatted in pain, losing all his strength. And there the mountain settled, squashing the mouse beneath it.

From that day on, the people called the mountain Afsynakhak—Mouse.

That's all. The end.

Мышонок и сопка

ак, говорят, бало. В конце чаплинской косы, за озером, не было раньше никакой сопки. И вдруг появилась. Назвали люди эту сопку Афсынахак — Мышонок. А произошло всё вот как. Однажды маленький афсынахак, мышонок, призадумался: «Почему про людей сказки рассказывают и песни поют, а про наше мышиное племя ничего хорошего не услышишь? Люди богатырями бывают, колдунами, храбрыми охотниками, бегунами, прыгунами. А мыши не бывают. Что надо сделать, чтобы про меня и про мой мышиный род слава среди людей пошла? А ну-ка перегрызу я это высоченное дерево, взвалю на спину да подниму на верхушку сопки. Пусть люди увидят наконец мышиного богатыря!»

И начал мышонок перегрызать дерево, начал раскачивать его из стороны в сторону. Только дерево никак не падает. Ещё яростнее стал грызть, покачнулось дерево и упало. Обрадовался было мышонок, да увидел, что не дерево он повалил, а высокую травинку. Стыдно стало мышонку, неловко. Он подумал: «Хорошо, что соседи не видели, а то засмеяли бы! Но что же мне такое сделать, чтобы весь мир удивить?» И вот побежал он по тундре, а перед ним большущее озеро. Мышонок подумал: «Вот переплыву через это озеро, сяду на другом берегу, буду

сушить свою кухлянку, штаны и торбаза. Увидят меня люди и скажут: "Вот так пловец! Какое озеро переплыл!" Будут обо мне сказки рассказывать и песни петь".

И вот поплыл мышонок через озеро, чуть посредине не утонул. Еле-еле до другого берега доплыл, стал одежду сушить. Сидит на камешке, видит — человек идёт. Идёт и следы на сырой земле оставляет, а на месте каждого следа большое озеро появляется. "Вот, оказывается, через какое озеро я переплыл", —подумал мышонок, и так ему обидно стало, что такой он маленький!

Надел мышонок непросохшую одежду и отправился к круглой сопке. Остановился перед сопкой, вспомнил свои неудачи, да так рассердился, что чуть не заплакал. Подбежал тут мышонок к сопке, взвалил её сгоряча на спину и понёс в северную сторону. Нёс, нёс, устал. Посмотрел вперёд, а там посёлок Тыфляк виднеется. Мышонок подумал: "Зайду в Тыфляк, передохну. Увидят меня люди и скажут: "Ого, какой богатырь, сопку принёс!" Будут обо мне сказки рассказывать и песни петь!" Тряхнул мышонок сопку, чтобы удобнее нести. От сотрясения отвалился от сопки камешек да и угодил мышонку в голову. Присел мышонок от боли, силы потерял. Тут его сопка и придавила.

С тех пор эскимосы называют эту сопку Афсынахак-Мышонок.

Всё. Конец.

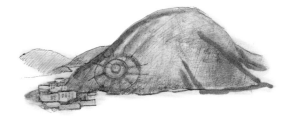

THE SMART VIXEN AND THE TEALS

ne day, the vixen was roaming along the lakeshore. She walked and walked until she came upon a *baydara*—a large open skin boat. Running to it, she ordered the oarsmen, "Look here, you row toward me right away and take me with you! I've walked a long time and I am very tired. Row here right away! You know what strength I have!"

Recognizing the smart vixen, the oarsmen replied, "Ege, you're such an important person and you travel on foot, while we, the nobodies, travel in a *baydara*. Come right away, sit with us!"

The oarsmen moored the *baydara* at the shore, and the smart vixen, with a proud look on her face, climbed in. She sat down in the middle of the *baydara*, folded her arms and legs, leaned back a little and, out of a sense of pure satisfaction, closed her eyes. They rowed farther. After just a little while, the *baydara* suddenly made a loud noise, rose up into the air, and the smart vixen found herself in the water!

What a miracle! The oarsmen turned out to be teals. It was they who had carried the vixen on their wings. The vixen felt cold all over, the chill reaching to her bones. Ay, ay, those teals tricked her! You know, it's not for nothing that they call her the smart vixen—but now the teals had turned out to be smarter.

The vixen looked back at her water-soaked tail, and exclaimed to it, "Help me, tail, to reach the shore. You know, if we don't reach dry land, we'll drown! Work harder, with all your might!"

Wet all over, the vixen almost sank. What had those teals done to her? Barely, barely, she reached dry land and climbed up onto a boulder. Looking down at herself, she didn't recognize what she saw. Somehow she had become a thin creature. All of her fur now clung to her, lying flat against her skin. The vixen got up on her feet and shook herself dry. Burning red with shame, she ran off into the tundra.

The end.

Лиса-хитрунья и чирки

днажды шла лиса вдоль берега. Шла, шла, байдару увидела. Повернулась в её сторону и говорит гребцам таким важным голосом:

«А ну-ка, плывите ко мне поскорее, возьмите меня с собой! Давно я иду, сильно устала. Скорее плывите сюда! Знаете ведь, какая у меня сила!»

Узнали гребцы лису-хитрунью и говорят ей:

«Эге, такой ты важный человек, а пешком идёшь, а мы, ничтожные, на байдаре едем. Иди скорее, садись к нам!»

Причалила байдара к берегу, полезла лиса-хитрунья с гордым видом в байдару. Села на середину байдары, руки-ноги скрестила, назад откинулась, от удовольствия глаза закрыла. Поплыли дальше. Немного погодя вдруг байдара зашумела и поднялась в воздух, а лиса-хитрунья в воде очутилась.

Что за чудеса! Байдарные гребцы утками-чирками оказались. Это они на своих крыльях лису везли. Почувствовала лиса холод во всем теле, до самых костей пробирает. Ай, ай, обманули её утки-чирки! Ведь, кажется, недаром её лиса-хитрунья зовут, а вот чирки похитрее оказались.

Повернулась лиса к своему намокшему хвосту и как закричит:

«Помоги мне, хвост, до берега доплыть, а то ведь не дотянем до суши, утонем! Уж давай, поднатужься!»

Намокла лиса, совсем погрузилась в воду. Вот ведь что чирки сделали! Едва-едва до суши добралась, на гальку выползла. Посмотрела на себя и не узнала. Как будто бы она какой-то тонкой тварью стала. Так её всю шерсть облепила. Встала лиса на ноги, встряхнулась, и что было сил от стыда в тундру побежала.

Конец.

THE WOMAN WITH THE BALL

hey say there was once a woman who lived in a big house, a nice house. She did not do any housework. All she did was play with a ball. One day, she went to sleep. In the morning, she got up, ate, and said, "Well, now I'm ready, I can go. I have a nice big ball to play with!"

She came out of the house. She began to kick the ball. She played with it all day. And when she got tired of playing with it, she went back home to rest a little.

Some time later, the woman asked herself, "Oh, what can I use to make myself a new ball? Will I even be able to do this? Yes, I will be able to do this—because I, you see, am not from here; I'm special—I'm a woman of the moon! She is my mother!"

The woman then took the moon and the sun and made herself a ball. She put the sun on one side of the ball and the moon on the other. The ball was ready, but there was nothing inside of it—it was empty. The woman said to herself, "What can I use to fill this ball? It's so big and nice!"

She went out, looked up, and said once again, "What can I use to fill my ball? Well, I will fill it with all those things. I will take all the stars from the heavens!"

She gathered all the stars from the heavens. Then she went back to the house, took the ball, filled it with the stars, and sewed it closed. When she was finished, she carried

61

the ball outdoors. Now there were no stars, no moon, and no sun in the sky. It was dark everywhere—pitch dark. The woman said, "Now, then, I will throw my ball up!"

She threw the ball up in the air, and immediately the sky became light. When the ball fell back to the ground, darkness returned. When she threw the ball up, light returned; when she caught it falling—dark. After she got tired of playing, she took the ball and went back inside. Outside, it remained pitch dark!

It was terrible for all people.

The men asked, "What is this? Where is the sun? Where are the moon and stars?" Hearing of this situation, an Inchoun man from far away thought for a while, then declared, "I will go on a trip with the dogs to find out what has happened to the heavens!"

He loaded his sled with two bags made of whole seal skins filled with fat. He harnessed the dogs. He took with him a long thick pole. He said, "So, this is what's happening! All the people are gloomy because there is no sun, no moon, and no stars. What if I go to Lorino? I will call on a sister who lives there."

As he left, he dipped the pole in the fat and lit it. Like a candle, it threw light on the path. There was no wind. All the way, he dipped the pole in the fat.

He was halfway through with the trip.

The woman inside the house with the ball saw him coming by and thought: "What kind of a man is this? How clever! He lights a candle and travels! Now I must go out. I can't help but have pity for such a man!"

She took the ball and went out. She threw the ball upwards. Suddenly there was light everywhere.

The man traveling to Lorino was frightened. After a while, he said to himself, "Well now, really! I think I know what happened to the sun, the moon, and the stars. So that's it! And a woman at that! Where did she come from? All the people could be wiped out. What should I do about her? It would be the right thing to take the ball from her!"

He walked toward her. The woman caught the ball and took it back inside the house. Again it became dark. The man came up to the house and shouted, "Hey there, woman! Come out!"

The woman answered, "I will not come out!"

The man repeated, "Really now, come out!"

The woman again said, "I will not come out!"

The man took out a stone knife. He pushed his way into the house and grabbed the woman, "Now I will kill you! How bad you are! Because of you, all of the people are dying. Now I will kill you!"

"Don't kill me!"

"I will!"

Frightened, the woman pleaded, "All right, I will throw the ball!"

The man said, "Then I will not kill you! Let's go!"

They went outside. The women threw the ball to the ground. The man told her, "No! Throw upwards! What have you done with the sun, the moon, and the stars? Cut the ball and then throw!"

The woman cried out, "Oy, oy, oy! Then I will be without a ball!"

She covered her face with her hands and sobbed.

The man picked up the ball and threw it high into the air. As he did so he exclaimed, "Ege!"

At once it became light.

The man said to the woman, "Do not do that again!"

The woman answered, "All right. I will not do that again."

The Inchoun man returned home. And the people were happy again. From that time on, the woman sewed and sewed. She made a ball and on it she sewed the sun, the moon, and the stars. She made many such balls.

That is all.

Женщина с мячом

оворят, женщина одна жила. Большой дом у женщины был, хороший. Не работала она. Вся её работа была — в мяч играть. Поспит женщина, утром проснётся, поест и говорит:

«Ну вот, я и готова, можно идти. Хороший у меня мяч, большой!»

Выйдет. Станет мяч пинать. Весь день в мяч играет. Устанет, в дом идёт отдохнуть.

Вот раз подумала женщина: «Ох, из чего же мне мяч новый сделать? Только, наверное, не сумею я. Да нет, пожалуй, сумею, потому что я ведь не здешняя, я ведь хорошая, лунная! Луна-то — моя мать!»

И вот взяла она луну, взяла солнце и сделала мяч. Солнце с одной стороны, луна — с другой. Готов мяч, только нет в нём ничего, пустой. Говорит женщина:

«Чем же мне наполнить мой мяч, такой большой и красивый!»

Вышла, посмотрела вверх и говорит:

«Чем же ещё наполнить мой мяч? Вот и наполню всем этим. Все звёзды с неба возьму!»

Собрала все звёзды с неба. Вошла в дом. Взяла мяч. Насыпала внутрь звёзд. Зашила мяч. Кончила дело, вышла. А на небе ни звёзд, ни луны, ни солнца нет.

Темно везде. Говорит женщина:

«А ну-ка, брошу я свой мяч вверх!»

Бросила. Сразу светло стало. Упал мяч — опять темнота кругом. Подбросит мяч — светло, поймает — темно. Кончила играть, взяла мяч, в дом пошла. Мяч с собой взяла. Такая кругом тьма стала, хоть глаз выколи!

Страшно людям стало. Мужчины говорят:

«Как же так? Где солнце? Где луна и звёзды?»

Один мужчина инчоунский задумался. Говорит:

«Отправлюсь-ка я в путь на собаках, на собачьей упряжке, узнаю, что случилось на небе!»

Погрузил на нарту два мешка из целых нерпичьих шкур, наполненных жиром, собак запряг. Взял бревно — длинное, толстое. Говорит:

«Вон что делается! Весь народ мрёт, потому что солнца нет, луны и звёзд нет. Поеду-ка я в Лорино. Хоть сестру, которая там живёт, поведаю».

Отправился. Макнёт в жир бревно, подожжёт, и горит свеча, дорогу освещает. А ветра совсем нет. Ну и безветрие! Так он всю дорогу макал бревно в жир.

Вот уже полпути проехал.

Увидела его женщина с мячом и говорит:

«Вот так мужчина! Какой умный! Зажёг свечу и едет! Сейчас выйду — жалко мне этого мужчину!»

Захватила с собой мяч и вышла. Подбросила мяч вверх. Вдруг кругом светло стало.

Испугался едущий в Лорино мужчина. А потом говорит:

«Вот так-как! Думаем, куда это солнце делось, куда луна и звёзды подевались? А оказывается, вон оно что! Ну и женщина! Откуда она взялась? Весь народ хочет погубить. Что мне с ней сделать? Хорошо бы мяч у нее отнять!»

Поехал к ней. Женщина снова в дом вошла. Опять темно стало. Подъехал мужчина к дому, говорит:

«Ну-ка, женщина, выходи!»

Женщина отвечает:

«Не выйду!»

Мужчина говорит:

«Нет уж, выходи!»

Женщина снова отвечает:

«Не выйду!»

Взял мужчина каменный нож. Вошёл. Схватил женщину, говорит:

«Сейчас я тебя убью! Какая ты плохая! Весь народ из-за тебя погибает. Сейчас убью!»

«Не убивай!»

«Убью!»

Испугалась женщина, говорит:

«Ладно, брошу я этот мяч!»

Мужчина в ответ:

«Тогда не убью! Пойдём!»

Вышли. Бросила женщина мяч на землю. Мужчина говорит ей:

«Нет, ты вверх бросай! Что ты сделала с солнцем, луной и звёздами? Разрежь-ка мяч и бросай!»

Женщина воскликнула:

«Ой, ой, ой! Осталась я без мяча!»

Прикрыла лицо руками, заплакала.

Бросил мужчина мяч высоко вверх. Только и крикнул при этом:

«Эгэ!»

Сразу стало светло.

Мужчина говорит:

«Больше так не делай!»

Женщина отвечает:

«Ладно. Не буду делать больше так».

Отправился инчоунский мужчина домой. Обрадовались все люди. А женщина с тех пор всё шила и шила. Сошьёт мяч — солнце, луну и звёзды на нём вышьет. Много мячей сшила.

Всё.

THE FORMATION
OF THE STRAIT

t is told that in the past, before the arrival of Europeans, the islands of Inetlin and Imeglin were one island out of which arose two mountains divided by a stream, over which had been placed a whale-bone bridge for crossing.

Eskimos lived on the island. They hunted many walrus and seals. Some kept reindeer in the tundra.

The richest of the herders, Tepkelin, was strong and successful. He had plenty to eat. His food storage pit was always filled with meat. He and his wife lived by themselves.

One day during the summer Tepkelin went hunting in a *kayak*. The weather was just fine. The ringed seals, *nerpas*, surfaced all around him, but Tepkelin did not harpoon them. He was waiting for the bearded seals, *lakhtaks*, to show up. When they did not appear, he rowed farther out into the open sea—so far that he soon could barely see the village.

Tepkelin stopped and waited for *lakhtaks* to show up. After some time, a large *lakhtak* appeared, surfacing in front of him, close to the *kayak*. At once, Tepkelin threw the harpoon. The harpoon head struck the *lakhtak* directly in the neck. Quickly, Tepkelin lowered a *poplavok*, an inflated *nerpa's* seal skin, into the water. The *lakhtak* dove and ran, but Tepkelin followed until the *lakhtak* gradually lost

strength. Finally, Tepkelin pulled the weakened *lakhtak* to the *kayak* and fastened him to the *poplavok*.

The sun was already setting. It was getting dark. Tepkelin paddled quickly toward the shore, but he was still far out to sea when the sun set.

Suddenly, some kind of animal jumped out of the sea and dug its claws into Tepkelin's back. Try as he may, Tepkelin could not tear the beast from his back. He kept rowing to the shore with all his might. The animal was tearing his *kukhlyanka*, a long pullover outer fur garment, to shreds! Tepkelin paddled faster and faster. The animal tore his *kukhlyanka* to pieces, down to his bare back. It began to tear at Tepkelin's skin. In pain, Tepkelin almost lost his oar.

He tried again and again to knock the animal off his back, but he could not—it held on. Blood began to run from his wounds. *Better get to the shore quicker—there will be help there!* The closer he got to the village, the more his strength increased, overcoming his pain. Now the land was near. People stood on the shore, waiting. Tepkelin began to weaken. As he neared land, he cried out to the people, "Some animal, I don't know what kind, is clinging to my back! Pull it from my back, but let it live!"

The point of the *kayak* touched the sand. At once, the people pulled the boat up onto dry land. Stuck to Tepkelin's back was some kind of animal unknown to them. Seeing all the people, the animal let go of Tepkelin and tried to rush back into the sea. Some of the villagers carried Tepkelin to his *yaranga*—a barrel-roofed dwelling. Others chased down and captured the animal. They went into the *yaranga*, where Tepkelin sat eating supper, his whole back covered with wounds. The people said to Tepkelin, "We have caught your tormentor! What should we do with it?"

Tepkelin told them to skin the beast and release it into the sea. They did as he desired.

Night came and all the people fell asleep. Even Tepkelin slept. During the night, he was awakened by the loud noise of nearby breakers—the breakers seemed very nearby. A strong wind had come up, blowing the waves into the lowlands around the village.

Tepkelin quickly put on his clothes and ran outside. The waves had already reached the first *yaranga* at the edge of the village. The people were gathering together to flee up to the mountains. Everywhere dogs howled, people screamed, the surf pounded. Seeing that the waves were about to reach his *yaranga*, Tepkelin ran inside and told his wife to gather herself to go to the mountains. He tarried just a bit. Suddenly, an enormous wave swooped over Tepkelin's *yaranga*. In its retreat, it carried all of the gathered villagers away. Thus perished Tepkelin and his wife in the depths of the sea.

The wind raged all night. Many people perished, many dogs drowned, *yarangas* were swept into the sea by the waves. Only one small corridor of flat land remained.

At dawn, the wind gained force. A fog crept in, covering the mountains in black clouds. But soon it became light and the wind died down.

The people who had managed to get to high ground stared down from the mountain through the fog, trying to see their village. When the sun came out, they found in its place the sea. The sea had swallowed the entire spit on which their village once sat.

 And so was the strait formed. The two mountains—Inetlin and Imeglin—remain to this day. Only they have become islands.

The end.

Образование пролива

оворят, в прошлом, когда ещё европейцев не знали, острова Инетлин и Имеглин одним островом были. Возвышались на том острове две горы, а между ними шла маленькая протока, через которую китовые позвонки для перехода были переброшены.

На том острове эскимосы жили. Много моржей и нерп добывали. Некоторые в тундре у хозяев оленей пасли.

Самый богатый хозяин был Тэпкэлин. Сильный был и удачливый. Много пищи имел. Погреб у него всегда был мясом заполнен. Они жили одни с женой.

Однажды летом охотился Тэпкэлин в каяке. Погода была очень хорошая. Вокруг то и дело выныривали нерпы-тюлени. Но Тэпкэлин не гарпунил их. Ждал, когда лахтаки-тюлени появятся. Не дождавшись лахтаков, дальше в открытое море направился. Скоро уже селение на берегу едва виднелось. Остановился Тэпкэлин, стал ждать, когда лахтаки появятся. Через некоторое время впереди большой лахтак показался. Совсем близко вынырнул. Тэпкэлин сразу бросил в него гарпун. Наконечник гарпуна прямо в шею лахтаку вошёл. Тэпкэлин быстро спустил на воду пузырь — надутую шкуру нерпы. Нырнул лахтак, а пузырь не пускает. Поплыл Тэпкэлин вслед за лахтаком. Стал лахтак

постепенно силы терять. Наконец подтянул Тэпкэлин ослабевшего лахтака к каяку и закрепил на пузыре.

Солнце уже спускалось. Темнеть стало. Тэпкэлин к берегу заспешил. Солнце село, когда он ещё далеко в море был.

Вдруг выскочил из воды какой-то зверь и впился когтями Тэпкэлину в спину. Не смог Тэпкэлин оторвать его от спины. Стал к берегу изо всех сил грести. А зверь давай кухлянку царапать. Тэпкэлин ещё сильнее заторопился. Разорвал зверь кухлянку, до спины добрался, стал кожу когтями рвать. Тэпкэлин от боли чуть не упустил весло.

Опять попробовал зверя от спины отодрать, не смог — крепко зверь вцепился. Из ран уже кровь течёт. Скорее бы до берега доплыть — только там спасение! Ещё сильнее стал Тэпкэлин грести, превозмогая боль. Вот уж близко земля. На берегу люди сидят, ждут. Очень ослабел Тэпкэлин. Как приблизился каяк к берегу, крикнул людям:

«Вцепился ко мне в спину неведомый зверь! Отдерите его от меня, только живым оставьте!»

Ткнулся нос каяка в песок, вытащили его люди тотчас на сушу. Видят — впился в спину Тэпкэлина какой-то неизвестный зверь. Отпустил зверь Тэпкэлина и бросился было к морю. Поймали его люди и отнесли Тэпкэлину в *ярангу*. А самого охотника ещё раньше туда отвели. Ужинает Тэпкэлин, а спина у него вся этим зверем изранена.

Говорят люди Тэпкэлину:

«Вот мы поймали твоего мучителя! Что нам теперь с ним сделать?»

Велел Тэпкэлин содрать с него шкуру и отпустить в море. Так они и сделали.

Наступила ночь, все люди уснули. И Тэпкэлин уснул. Проснулся ночью, слышит — шум прибоя совсем близко. Сильный ветер дует, а вокруг селения по низинам уже волны гуляют.

Быстро оделся Тэпкэлин и выбежал наружу. Волны уже до первых *яранг* докатились. Собираются люди на гору бежать. А вокруг собачий вой, крики людей, шум прибоя. Скоро волны и к *яранге* Тэпкэлина подступили. Тэпкэлин вбежал в *ярангу*, велел жене собираться, на гору идти. Только немного замешкался. Накатилась огромная волна, разбила *ярангу* и утащила вместе с людьми в море. Погибли Тэпкэлин с женой в морской пучине.

Всю ночь бушевал ветер. Много людей погибло, много собак утонуло, *яранги* волнами в море смыло. Маленькая полоска земли только осталась.

На рассвете ещё сильнее стал ветер. Наступила мгла. Горы заволокло тучами. Но вскоре посветлело. Ветер стал утихать.

Оставшиеся в живых люди смотрели с горы в сторону своего селения. Взошло солнце, и увидели они на его месте море. Всю косу, где селение было, поглотили волны.

Так вот образовался пролив. А две горы — Инетлин и Имеглин — и сейчас есть. Только они островами стали.

Конец.

THE MOUSE AND THE MARMOT

s a mouse was carousing between hummocks, a marmot sat, as usual, on a small nearby hillock yelling out, "Sik-sik, sik-sik, sik-sik." Hearing the marmot, the mouse seated herself on a hummock and called out to her, "Hello stranger! Come here!"

As the marmot approached, the mouse shouted, "Welcome!"

"Welcome!" replied the marmot.

The mouse then said to the marmot, "You know, since we have to live together, shouldn't we go hunting bears together?"

"Oh, no. The bear is too frightening! We'll not kill him. He will surely kill us!"

But the mouse insisted. "Don't worry. We'll outsmart him. We're very small—we'll sneak up on him and scratch him to death."

The marmot thought a little. "All right, let's do it!"

The mouse and the marmot went off together to hunt a bear, and it wasn't long before they found one. Sneaking up on him, they were drawing quite near when the mouse cried out to the marmot, "Oy-oy-oy, he really is a fright!"

The marmot retorted, "Didn't I just tell you that? He is a fright!"

Hearing this, the bear shouted out, "I'll eat you!"

They then called back to him, "Hey, grandpa, we have something to tell you. Listen to us! Do you have fleas?"

The bear replied, "Oh, to be sure. I have many!"

"Let us search for them!"

"All right, search!"

The marmot and the mouse climbed up onto the bear and began searching for fleas. As they were combing through his thick fur, the bear dozed off to sleep. Hearing the bear's soft snore, the mouse whispered to the marmot, "Now, let's scratch his eyes out! Maybe we'll even kill him!"

They scratched out the bear's eyes; they scratched them to pieces. The fluid ran out of them. Then blood ran out. And more blood, until the bear was dead.

The marmot and the mouse congratulated each other. "Oh, how strong we are—we've killed the bear! From now on, let's do things together. When we're together, even the bear is not such a fright!"

The end.

Мышка и евражка

уляла мышка между кочек, а евражка сидела, как обычно, на холмике и кричала:

«Сык-сык, сык-сык, сык-сык».

Услышала мышка, как она кричит, села на кочку. Позвала евражку:

«Дядя, иди сюда!»

Евражка подошла. Мышка говорит ей:

«Здравствуй!»

«Здравствуй!»

Мышка сказала евражке:

«А что, если нам вместе жить и вместе на медведей охотиться?»

«Ох нет, медведь-то страшилище! Не мы его, а он нас убьёт!»

Мышка возразила ей:

«Ничего, перехитрим его. Мы очень маленькие, подкрадёмся к нему и зацарапаем его до смерти».

Евражка подумала и сказала:

«Ну ладно, давай!»

As the snowstorm continued to rage, the calf, not yet licked clean by his mother, tried to get up, but could not. The next day it cleared. Somewhat encouraged, the calf crawled over to his mother. He sucked a little—he was very careful with the milk. Every time he felt hungry he sucked just a little. And the calf became stronger. He ran around his mother and learned how to run fairly fast.

The calf stayed there by himself, all the time running around his mother; he wanted to become very fast at running. Spring came and he continued to run all the time. Summer arrived and he began to run in wider circles, always at a trot. But he always returned to his mother. In this way, the young deer prepared himself for the arrival of the wolf, at the same time asking himself: "Why should I let him eat me when I could run away?"

Fall arrived. Suddenly the wolf appeared and asked of the young deer, "Well, can I kill you now?"

"That would be a pity," replied the young deer. "I'm still small and skinny. You would not get much to eat!"

"It seems you are right. I will not eat you now, but I'll return again next year. Don't go anywhere from here. Wait for me!" said the wolf.

"All right. Go!" said the young deer.

Again he exercised by running. He went all over the mountains. Winter came. The young deer learned to run ever faster.

Another year went by. The young deer grew some more. Again the wolf appeared. He asked, "Well, what's with you now?"

"I'm trying to fatten myself," the young deer answered.

"That's good of you," said the wolf. "But when do I get to eat you?"

"It's a pity that I'm not big and fat yet!"

"That's for certain. Then I will come in a year," said the wolf.

"Very well. Go!"

Again the wolf went off into the tundra.

The young deer never thought of getting fat; he only wanted to become stronger and faster. For that, he practiced running all year.

And so another year went by. The wolf appeared and asked, "Well, no doubt you've become good and fat?"

"I don't know why, but it seems I'm still skinny. I just don't seem to be able to grow fat!"

"Really? Well, so be it. I'll come back in a year!"

Once again the wolf went off into the tundra.

The young deer again exercised all year—he ran over the mountains and jumped from cliffs.

Another year went by. Again, the wolf appeared. He said to the young deer, "Now, to be sure, you must be a fully proper meal!"

"Well, I've grown, but I'm still skinny. It was a bad year. I did not get fat!"

"That seems to be the case. You are indeed painfully skinny," said the wolf. "Well, I'll leave, but for the last time."

"All right, go!"

Actually, the deer tricked the wolf—he did not want to get fat.

Winter came. The deer ran all the time. He jumped from cliffs, giving himself a good workout every day.

Again summer arrived. He walked alone in the mountains. He began to resemble a mountain goat—strong and limber. He jumped from low cliffs and butted boulders, gaining greater and greater strength. But because he didn't have a mountain goat's horns, he came to be called Akannykay, meaning "Bad Antlers."

No matter how far Akannykay roamed, he always returned to that place where his mother had been killed by the wolf. He always came home to the bones of his mother.

There, the wolf again found him. This time, the wolf was very hungry.

Akannykay said to him, "Ah, welcome! You've arrived?"

"Yes, I've arrived," the wolf answered. "And I'm now ready to eat you!"

The deer agreed, "So what? If you wish, it is now possible!"

But really he did not think that way. You see, he had become very big, strong, and agile.

The wolf said, "Well then, let me kill you and eat you!" He was ready for a good meal.

Then Akannykay said to the wolf, "How about I just run a little ways away from you? I will just run a little! Why hand myself over right away?"

The wolf agreed, "Very well... Run!" He believed he would have little trouble catching the deer.

And so Akannykay ran. He ran very fast. The wolf darted after him up the mountain. No way could he catch up with him. The deer slowed, and the wolf come nearer. Akannykay slowed more, and the wolf drew even closer. It turned out the Akannykay was leading the wolf to a high cliff.

At last, the wolf cried out, "You wait! Didn't you say that you were not going to run far?"

"Catch up with me!" Akannykay cried out in answer, as they approached a cliff.

At the edge of the cliff, the deer jumped down. The wolf, following close behind and thinking he had finally caught up with the deer, leaped off the cliff after him. And you know it was a high cliff! Below ran a wide river. Akannykay swam across, while the wolf tumbled down the mountain like a boulder and came to a stop on the riverbank. He had hurt his legs badly.

The wolf yelped, "O-o-y! Oy, it is so painful! May all your enemies gnaw you to the bone! May you die in pain and misery, you orphan!"

"Serves you right! Why did you kill my mother? I will yet settle accounts with you, wolf!" cried Akannykay.

"All right, settle accounts for your mother! But I will call on my companions," the wolf called out to Akannykay from where he lay at the base of the tall cliff.

"All right then, invite your friends!" answered Akannykay. "I also have friends!"

Akannykay asked a hare and an ermine to help him.

A large pack of wolves came to help the injured wolf.

Lying injured below the cliff, the wolf said to his companions, "Let's kill that deer Akannykay! Run after him! When you catch up to him, kill him at once! And think of the most painful way of doing it. Do you understand?"

"Yes, we do," they answered.

Before they could leave, others showed up to help: a wolverine, brown bear, arctic foxes, mice, marmots, gulls, vixens, and an old wild deer—a very big one. This old wild deer was known as Bad-Match. But his real name was Matachgyrkynaynyn, which means "the son of a bad match." His body was like that of a deer, but his feet resembled those of a dog. Also, he had antlers—such big antlers that they blocked the sun. But Akannykay had no fear of the old deer with dog's feet.

Only those two friends, the hare and the ermine, came forward to help Akannykay. Meanwhile, the wolf dispatched his army and said, "Well now, go and catch up with him!"

They headed out.

The mice followed directly in the footsteps of the deer, while the others made their way through the grass. All were anxious to challenge the deer.

All of a sudden, Bad-Match began to run fast, and then faster. He ran so fast, he was far ahead of Akannykay. As he ran, the air behind him swirled up like a snowstorm. It became impossible to see him!

The herd of wolf helpers ran along for a long time; then they drifted apart—some were fast runners, but others couldn't keep up. Try as they may, even the gulls were no match for Bad-Match. He outran everybody. Left behind, the wolf's helpers started to give up and go home.

Then Akannykay said to the hare and the ermine, "Now, let's try to catch up to Bad-Match! We can't let him outrun us!"

"By all means, let's do that!" said his friends.

The hare and the ermine attached themselves to Akannykay's legs, and he carried them along with him.

Oh, and how fast he ran! Much faster than Bad-Match! Akannykay appeared to be flying. It looked like his feet were not even touching the ground.

They began to draw closer to Bad-Match. Bad-Match created such a swirling wind! Suddenly, it was as if they were inside a big snowstorm—but the weather had been fine that day!

Then Akannykay said to his friends, "All right, now let's catch up to Bad-Match!"

Bursting through that storm, Akannykay caught and killed Bad-Match.

Meanwhile, behind them, a bear, the strongest of the wolf's friends, approached.

"Let me try to best the bear," the ermine offered.

"Try," agreed Akannykay.

The ermine threw himself at the bear. They began to fight. The ermine jumped far and wide.

Suddenly, the bear lost track of the ermine. He hadn't noticed that the ermine had jumped into his mouth.

The bear said to himself: "Where did he go?"

Then, suddenly, the bear started spinning from pain, "Oy! Oy-oy!" he screamed. He rolled on the ground and cried out some more. In the end, he died.

Climbing out of the bear's mouth, the ermine told Akannykay, "I jumped into his mouth. Then I let myself farther into his stomach. Then I began to gnaw. Because I did so, I killed the bear fast."

Akannykay was impressed and proud of his friend. "Thanks to you for destroying such a big enemy!"

He would have liked to stay there longer, congratulating the ermine, but, looking up, he suddenly exclaimed, "The gulls are still left!"

Akannykay jumped up into the air, grabbed the gulls, and twisted their wings off. And he killed all of them. He then stamped all of the mice to death. He easily got rid of the foxes and all the others.

There remained alive only the one lone limping wolf.

Akannykay approached him, "Now, you're the only one left to talk with. Why did you kill my dear mother in such a snowstorm? You know, it was so hard for me—I had just been born. I've never forgotten how you humiliated me. You are a glutton, wolf!"

At last, Akannykay began to feel all of his anger.

"Did you really think every year that I would make myself fat for you? It wasn't so! All I wanted was to get stronger, more limber, and faster so that I could one day take my revenge on you!"

Akannykay then killed the wolf.

He turned to his friends. "Thank you for helping me! Now we will all live together in peace and harmony."

The end.

Аканныкай-Плохорогонький

говорят, была дикая важенка. И жила она совершенно одна. Всю зиму по горам ходила. К весне пришло время телиться. А ещё снег не стаял. Ещё завывала пурга.

Вот в пургу и отелилась в горах.

Облизывала мать телёночка, а тут волк подкрался и набросился на неё. Ох и сильно важенка отбивалась, но не смогла вырваться. И волк убил её. А телёночек, ещё не облизанный, в пурге остался мёрзнуть.

Волчище уже доедал важенку. Тут телёночек попросил его:

«Хоть вымя оставь, чтобы я мог вырасти, молоком питаясь!»

«Ну что ж, всё равно ведь мне на еду достанешься!» —сказал волк.

«Ладно!» —согласился телёнок.

«Что ж, пожалуй, оставлю! Но только на следующий год приду за тобой. Никуда не уходи, тут и жди меня!» —сказал волк.

«Не уйду, здесь буду, пока ты не явишься!» —обещал телёнок.

Ушёл волк в глубь тундры.

И вот в самую пургу телёнок, ещё матерью не облизанный, хочет встать и не может. На следующий день прояснилось. Приободрился немного телёнок,

Tamara 2011

подполз к матери. Пососал немного — очень берёг молоко. Всякий раз, как чувствует голод, сосёт понемногу. И начал телёнок крепнуть. Вертится вокруг матери, стал уже довольно быстро бегать. Так и жил один. Всё время вокруг матери бегал — очень ему хотелось быстрым стать. Наступила весна, а он так всё и бегает. Лето пришло — подальше стал бегать и всё время рысью. Но к матери всегда возвращался. Так и готовился оленёнок к приходу волка. При этом думал: «Ни за что ему меня не съесть — убегу!»

Пришла осень, вдруг явился волчище и спросил оленёнка:

«Ну что, можно убивать тебя?»

«Вот жаль — я ещё маленький и худой, не наешься!» —ответил оленёнок.

«Ты, пожалуй, прав. Не съем я тебя сейчас, но на следующий год опять вернусь. Никуда отсюда не уходи, дожидайся меня!» —сказал волк.

«Ладно, иди!» —сказал оленёнок.

И опять в беге упражняется. Все горы исходил. Наступила зима. Оленёнок ещё быстрее стал бегать.

Опять год прошёл. Оленёнок ещё подрос. Снова волк явился. Спрашивает:

«Ну а теперь как?»

«Да вот всё зажиреть стараюсь», —отвечает молодой олень.

«Что ж, спасибо тебе, —сказал волк. —Но когда же я тебя съем?»

«Вот жаль, что я всё ещё не такой большой и жирный!»

«Да, конечно. Тогда я через год приду», —сказал волк.

«Ладно, иди!»

Опять волк отправился в тундру.

А молодой олень совсем и не думал жиреть, а хотел стать сильным и быстрым. Для этого весь год в беге упражнялся.

И вот опять прошёл год, явился волк и спросил:

«Ну, теперь-то уж, наверное, хороший стал, жирный?»

«Не знаю, только, по-моему, я все ещё худой. Никак не могу вырасти и пожиреть».

«И в самом деле. Пожалуй, я ещё через год приду!»

Опять волк в тундру ушёл.

И вот опять молодой олень весь год упражняется: бегает по горам, прыгает с обрывов.

Прошёл ещё год, опять явился волк. Говорит молодому оленю:

«Ну теперь-то ты, наверное, вполне подходящей пищей стал!»

«Вырасти-то вырос, да вот худоват ещё. Плохой год был, не зажирел!» —ответил олень.

«А ведь и правда, больно худой, —сказал волк. —Ну, уйду пока».

«Ладно, иди!»

А на самом-то деле олень обманывал волка — не старался жиреть.

Наступила зима. Олень всё время бегает, с обрывов прыгает, каждый день упражняется.

Опять лето пришло. Стал он только по горам ходить. Как горные бараны стал — крепкий и ловкий. С невысоких скал прыгал, каменные глыбы бодал. Большую силу приобрёл. И назвали его Аканныкай-Плохорогонький.

Где только ни бегал Аканныкай, но всегда на то место приходил, где волк его мать убил, всегда к материнским костям возвращался.

И вот опять встретил его волк. Очень он был в ту пору голодный.

Сказал ему Аканныкай:

«А, здравствуй! Пришёл?»

«Да, пришёл, — ответил волк. — Ну теперь-то уж тебя съем!»

Согласился олень:

«Что ж, теперь, пожалуй, можно!»

А на самом-то деле он не так думал. Ведь огромный стал, очень сильный и ловкий.

Волк и говорит:

«Ну, давай уж убью я тебя и съем!» — Очень хотелось волку есть.

Аканныкай отвечает:

«Только давай я сначала побегу от тебя! Немного так пробегу! Зачем же сразу сдаваться?»

Волк согласился:

«Ладно уж, беги!» — Он то был уверен, что сразу догонит.

И вот побежал Аканныкай. Очень быстро бежит. Бросился за ним волк, никак не может догнать. Подпустил олень волка поближе. А тот уже совсем медленно бежит.

Аканныкай-то, оказывается, волка к высокой скале завлекает.

Наконец закричал волк:

«Да подожди ты! Ведь говорил, что недалеко отбежишь!»

«А ты догоняй!» — крикнул в ответ Аканныкай.

Вот подбежали к скале. Олень прыгнул вниз. И волк за ним — думал поймать. А скала-то у самой реки была! Переплыл Аканныкай эту реку. А волк, как кочка, на берег упал. Крепко ноги зашиб. Как же, ведь высокая была скала!

Ну и взвыл волк:

«О-о-й! Ой, больно-то как! Да чтоб тебя до костей обглодали, сирота!»

«Так тебе и надо! Зачем мою матушку убил? Ещё не так за неё с тобой рассчитаюсь!» — крикнул Аканныкай.

«Ладно, рассчитывайся за мать! А я вот своих товарищей позову!» —закричал волк, лежа у подножия скалы, куда свалился.

«Ну ладно, зови своих товарищей! —отозвался Аканныкай. —И у меня они есть!»

Позвал Аканныкай на помощь зайца да горностая.

А волку на помощь большая волчья стая пришла.

Лежит волчище под скалой и говорит своим товарищам:

«Давайте убьём этого оленя Аканныкая! Сначала в беге и в борьбе с ним посостязаетесь, а как победите, то сразу же и убейте. Самую мучительную смерть ему придумать надо. Поняли?»

«Да, поняли», —ответили товарищи волка.

Кроме волчьей стаи пришла к волку на помощь росомаха, бурый медведь, песцы, мыши, евражки, чайки-разбойники, лисицы и один старый дикий олень, очень большой. Имя его было Матачгыркынайнын—сват-кобелище. Но у него только туловище было оленье, а ноги, как у собаки. Однако у него и рога были, да такие огромные, что закрывали солнце. Но Аканныкай не боялся этого оленя на собачьих ногах.

У Аканныкая было только два товарища — заяц и горностай.

Сказал волк своим помощникам:

«Ну, так отправляйтесь состязаться!»

И вот вышли.

Мыши прямо по следу оленя побежали, а другие помощники в траве пробирались. Все пошли состязаться.

Матачгыркынайнын сразу же быстро побежал. Бежит, а за ним вихрь клубится, подобно пурге. Даже его самого не видно.

Очень долго бежали. В пути кое-кто отстал: одни побыстрее бежали, другие — помедленнее. Чайки-разбойники изо всех сил старались от Матачгыркынайнына не отставать. Всё равно он их обогнал.

Стали помощники волка обратно поворачивать. И тут сказал Аканныкай товарищам:

«А ну-ка, попробуем догнать Матачгыркынайнына! Ведь нельзя же допустить, чтобы он нас перегнал!»

«Конечно, давайте!» —поддержали его товарищи.

Прыгнули заяц с горностаем под мышки Аканныкаю. Так и побежал с ними Аканныкай.

Ох и быстро бежал! Гораздо лучше, чем Матачгыркынайнын! Если смотреть на него сбоку, то как будто по воздуху летит Аканныкай!

И вот догнали Матачгыркынайнына. Как будто в пургу попали. А ведь очень

была хорошая погода. Это Матачгыркынайнын своим бегом создавал такой вихрь.

Тут сказал Аканныкай товарищам:

«Ну, теперь давайте перегоним Матачгыркынайнына!»

Ворвался Аканныкай в этот вихрь и убил Матачгыркынайнына.

Теперь только один медведь осталcя.

Горностай предложил:

«А ну-ка, давай я попробую с медведем справиться!»

«Попробуй», — согласился Аканныкай.

Бросился горностай на медведя. Начали бороться. Очень высоко и далеко горностай прыгал.

Вдруг потерял медведь горностая. Не заметил, как тот ему в рот прыгнул.

Говорит медведь:

«Куда же он делся?»

Затем вдруг завертелся от боли:

«Ой! Ой-ой!»

Катается по земле. Вот наконец умер. Вылез горностай изо рта медведя и рассказал Аканныкаю:

«Прыгнул я в рот, потом дальше в желудок спустился. Ну и начал грызть. Вот потому так быстро и убил медведя».

Сказал ему Аканныкай:

«Ну, спасибо тебе, что такого большого противника уничтожил!»

Хотел было и себя похвалить, да вспомнил:

«Ещё чайки-разбойники остались!»

Подпрыгнул вверх, повыкрутил им крылья. И убил всех. Мышей всех ногами затоптал. С песцами и всеми другими тоже легко справился.

Остался только один волк в живых.

Настиг его Аканныкай.

«Ну вот, только с тобой осталось поговорить. Зачем ты в такую пургу убил мою матушку? Ведь мне было так трудно тогда — только я родился. Не забыл я и как ты надо мной издевался. Обжора, волчище!»

Очень рассердился Аканныкай:

«Ты что же, думал, я каждый год буду для тебя жиреть? Как бы не так. Я хотел только сильным, ловким и быстрым стать. Всё для того, чтобы расквитаться с тобой!»

И убил тут Аканныкай злого волка.

Затем сказал товарищам:

«Спасибо вам, что помогли мне! Теперь будем все вместе жить, дружно и хорошо».

Конец.

NOTES AND ANNOTATIONS

How Swan Found Happiness

This fable was written by Alexander Dolitsky in December of 2009, in accordance with the style and motifs of the northern oral narratives. The concept of a floating feather in this fable was adapted by the author from Dmitriy Nagishkin's tale "Seven Fears," in which the main character of the story, Indiga, follows an eagle's feather in search of his lost brother, Solomdiga.

Как лебедь счастье нашёл

Сказака написана Александром Б. Долицким в стиле и по мотивам устного творчества коренных народов севера. Декабрь 2009 г.

The Quarrel between Sun and Moon

The fable was written by Alexander Dolitsky in August 2010, in accordance with the style and motifs of the northern oral narratives.

Спор солнца и луны

Сказака написана Александром Б. Долицким в стиле и по мотивам устного творчества коренных народов севера. Август 2010 г.

The Two Strongmen and the Oldster

The tale was told in 1960 by an inhabitant of Chaplino village, A. Algalik, age 40, recorded and translated into Russian by Georgiy A. Menovshchikov, and published in Russian by Georgiy A. Menovshchikov in *Skazki i mify narodov Chukotki i Kamchatki* (Fairy Tales and Myths of the People of Chukotka and Kamchatka), 1974, pp. 174-5. It was translated from Russian into English by Henry N. Michael and edited by Alexander Dolitsky in *Tales and Legends of the Yupik Eskimos of Siberia*, 2000, p. 103. This is a magical tale about two strongmen suckled by animals.

Kigi (or in Chukchi "Kikhi")—Arakamchechen Island in the Senyavin Strait, Bering Sea.

Ettuvi—a Chukchi name meaning "of a dog."

Yanrakinot is the Russian adaptation of the name of the Chukchi settlement of Yanrakynnot ("Stronghold") on the shore of the Senyavin Strait, Bering Sea.

Kaynuvi—a Chukchi name meaning "of the wild deer."

Baydara—an open skin boat with a light frame of driftwood and covered with split walrus hide (Eskimo: *umiak*). *Baydaras* were the principal means of travel among the Coastal Chukchi. The large *baydara* with sails was used for open-sea hunting of whales and walrus and for carrying goods along the coast.

Poplavok (Russian)—a hunting float used among the coastal dwellers of Chukotka and Kamchatka, consisting of a tightly sewn and inflated bladder or skin of a *nerpa* (ringed seal). It was tied to the harpoon with a long leather thong and kept the location of a harpooned sea mammal in sight of the pursuers.

Два силача и старик

Рассказал в 1960 году чаплинский житель А. Альгалик, 40 лет; записал и перевёл на русский язык Г.А. Меновщиков. Опубликована в книге *Сказки и мифы народов Чукотки и Камчатки*, 1974:174-5. Волшебная сказка о двух силачах, вскормленных животными.

Киги (или Кихи, чук.)—остров Аракамчечен в проливе Сенявина, Беренгово Море.

Этувьи («Собачий»)—чукотское имя.

Янракинот—русская адаптация названия чукотского посёлка Янракыннот («Твердыня») на побережье пролива Сенявина, Беренгово Моря.

Кайнувьи («Олений»)—чукотское имя.

Байдара—эскимосская лодка, сделанная из лёгкого деревянного каркаса, обтянутого моржовой шкурой.

Поплавок—у приморских жителей Чукотки и Камчатки поплавок представлял собой цельноснятую и надутую шкуру нерпы. Привязывался к гарпунному ремню и удерживал загарпуненного зверя на поверхности воды.

The Raven and the Owl

The tale was told in 1948 by the Eskimo, Ytoyuk, age 37, recorded and translated into Russian by Georgiy A. Menovshchikov, and published in Russian by Georgiy A. Menovshchikov in *Skazki i mify narodov Chukotki i Kamchatki* (Fairy Tales and Myths of the People of Chukotka and Kamchatka), 1974, pp. 193-94. It was translated from Russian into English by Henry N. Michael and edited by Alexander Dolitsky in *Tales and Legends of the Yupik Eskimos of Siberia*, 2000, p. 118. A variant of this tale was written by the Eskimo, Ermen, age 25, who had heard it rendered by his grandfather, Ivek, age 75. This ethnological tale is about a raven and an owl changing their appearance by painting each other. A similar theme is found among the Yukaghirs, the Greenlandic and North American Eskimos, the Japanese, and Vietnamese. In the Vietnamese tale with the same theme, in place of the owl there appears a peacock.

Zhirnik (Russian)—an oil lamp made of stone or, more rarely, of clay; used for light, heat, or cooking. The wick was made of twisted fur. Fat of different animals was usually used as fuel for *zhirnik*.

Ворониха и совиха

Рассказал в 1948 г. Председатель науканского колхоза эскимос Утоюк, 37 лет; записал и перевёл на русский язык Г.А. Меновщиков. Вариант этой сказки записан от эскимоса Эрмена, 25 лет, слышавшего её от своего деда Ивека, 75 лет. Опубликована впервые в книге *Сказки и мифы народов Чукотки и Камчатки*, 1974:193-94. Этиологическая сказка о том, как ворониха и сова покрасили друг друга. Сходный сюжет зафиксирован у юкагиров, гренландских и американских эскимосов, японцев и вьетнамцев (во вьетнамской сказке с тем же сюжетом вместо совы выступает павлин). *Японские сказки*, М., 1958, стр. 105; *Сказки и легенды Вьетнама*, М., 1958, стр. 176.

Жирник—сосуд жирового светильника, изготоввлявшийся из глины или из камня. Фителём служил толчёный сухой мох.

The Mouse and the Mountain

The tale was spoken in 1941 by an inhabitant of Naukan village, Uvrolyuk, age 22, recorded and translated into Russian by Georgiy A. Menovshchikov, and published in Russian by Georgiy A. Menovshchikov in *Skazki i mify narodov Chukotki i Kamchatki* (Fairy Tales and Myths of the People of Chukotka and Kamchatka), 1974, pp. 194-95. It was translated from Russian into English by Henry N. Michael and edited by Alexander Dolitsky in *Tales and Legends of the Yupik Eskimos of Siberia*, 2000, p. 119. Reflected in this tale is a toponymic legend about the name of the Afsynakhak—("*Myshonok*"—Little Mouse) Mountain. This tale did not become widespread and is known only by the Chaplino Eskimos, among whom, at that time, lived the Naukan Eskimo, Uvrolyuk. Afsynakhak Mountain is located near Chaplino hot springs.

Chaplino is a traditional Yupik Eskimo and Chukchi village in the Chukchi Peninsula of the Russian Far East.

Kukhlyanka is a long pullover outer fur garment. The combination of inner and outer fur shirts.

Torbaza is a footgear of seal skin or *kamus*. Winter *torbaza* were made of thick skins, usually from the lower part of reindeer legs, with the fur outside. Summer *torbaza* were made of the rawhide of seal throats.

Мышонок и сопка

Рассказал в 1941 г. житель села Наукан Увролюк, 22 лет. Записал и перевёл Г.А. Меновщиков. Опубликована в книге *Сказки и мифы народов Чукотки и Камчатки*, 1974:194-95. Отраженная в этой сказке топонимическая легенда о названии сопки Афсынахак («Мышонок») не получила распространения и зафиксирована только у чаплинских эскимосов, где жил в это время науканский эскимос Увролюк. Сопка Афсынахак находится около Чаплинских горячих ключей.

Кухлянка—верхняя меховая одежда.

Торбаза—обувь из нерпичьей шкуры или камусов (шкурок с оленьих ног).

The Smart Vixen and the Teals

The tale was narrated in 1948 by an inhabitant of Naukan village, Erman, age 23, recorded and translated into Russian by Georgiy A. Menovshchikov, and published in Russian by Georgiy A. Menovshchikov in *Skazki i mify narodov Chukotki i Kamchatki* (Fairy Tales and Myths of the People of Chukotka and Kamchatka), 1974, pp. 203-04. It was translated from Russian into English by Henry N. Michael and edited by Alexander Dolitsky in *Tales and Legends of the Yupik Eskimos of Siberia*, 2000, p. 129. The Naukan Eskimos, Kutvenun and Yaeka, recorded two variants of this tale in 1948-1949, as told. The theme of this tale is widespread over the entire Chukotka-Kamchatka region. While in the Eskimo tale the vixen is tricked by the teal ducks who throw her into the water, in the Itelmen tale with the same theme, the vixen is thrown from a raft capsized by gulls. Having reached the shore, the vixen, in this and the other variants, dries her fur and eyes. Further, in the Itelmen variant there begin the adventures of the vixen with the mocking Kutkho and the miraculous berries that pick themselves. The Itelmen theme of the tale is contaminated by other themes, while the Eskimo version stands by itself.

Vixen is a female fox. This word is used as a metaphor to describe an ill-tempered, shrewish, or malicious woman.

Лиса-хитрунья и чирки

Рассказал в 1948 г. житель села Наукан Эрмен, 23 лет. Записал и перевёл на русский язык Г.А. Меновщиков. Два варианта этой сказки были записаны в 1948-1949 гг. от науканских эскимосов Кутвенун и Яека. Сказка опубликована впервые в книге *Сказки и мифы народов Чукотки и Камчатки*, 1974:203-04. Сюжет этой сказки распространён по всему чукотско-камчатскому региону. Если в эскимосской сказке лису обманывают утки-чирки, сбросившие её в воду с лодки из крыльев, то в ительменской сказке на этот сюжет лису перевертывают с плотом чайки. Выбравшись на берег, лиса в том и другом вариантах просушивает шкуру и глаза. В ительменском варианте далее начинаются приключения лисы с насмешником Кутхом и чудесными ягодами, которые сами себя собирают. Ительменский сюжет этой сказки контаминируется с другими сюжетами, тогда как в эскимосском он бытует самостоятельно.

The Woman with the Ball

This tale was narrated in 1948 by an inhabitant of Uelen village in the Chukotsky region. The tale was recorded and translated into Russian by P. Skorik and published in Russian by Georgiy A. Menovshchikov in *Skazki i mify narodov Chukotki i Kamchatki* (Fairy Tales and Myths of the People of Chukotka and

Kamchatka), 1974, pp. 221-23. It was translated from Russian into English by Henry N. Michael and edited by Alexander Dolitsky in *Fairy Tales and Myths of the Bering Strait Chukchi*, 1997, pp. 10-11. In this rendering of the myth, the role of the cultural hero who returns the sun and the moon to the people is a human being. In the majority of other myths about the creation of the world, the sun, and the moon, the role of cultural heroes is played by birds—the raven and wagtail, and by animals—the hare. The subject of returning the sun has multiple parallels in the raven tales of the North American Indians.

The portrayal of the sun on handballs among the Chukchi and Siberian Yupik Eskimos is associated with myths about the abduction and return of heavenly bodies.

Inchoun—from a settlement the Chukchi call Inchuvin. The latter is derived from the Eskimo name for the same place, Insigvik.

Lorino—Russian adaptation of the name of the Chukchi settlement, Luren.

Женщина с мячом

Рассказал в 1948 г. житель села Уэлен Чукотского района Уватагын, 62 лет; записал и перевёл П.Я. Скорик. Сказка опубликована впервые в книге *Сказки и мифы народов Чукотки и Камчатки*, 1974:221-23. Миссию культурного героя, возвращающего людям солнце и луну, в этом мифическом предании исполняет человек. В большинстве же других мифов о происхождении света, солнца и луны культурными героями выступают птицы—ворон и трясогузка, и звери—заяц. Сюжет возвращения солнца имеет многочисленные параллели в сказаниях о вороне также у индейцев Северной Америки. Изображение солнца на ручных мячах у чукчей и азиатских эскимосов связано с мифами о похищении и возвращении небесных светил.

Изображение солнца на ручных мячах у чукчей и азиатских эскимосов связано с мифами о похищении и возвращении небесных светил.

Инчоунский—от чукотского названия селения Инчувин, восходящего к эскимосскому названию этой местности — Инсигвик.

Лорино—русская адаптация чукотского названия села Лурэн («Видимое жильё»).

The Formation of the Strait

The tale was narrated in 1948 by an inhabitant of Yandagay settlement in Chukotskiy region, Pakayka, age 62. The story was recorded and translated into Russian by P. Skorik and published in Russian by Georgiy A. Menovshchikov in *Skazki i mify narodov Chukotki i Kamchatki* (Fairy Tales and Myths of the People of Chukotka and Kamchatka), 1974, pp. 223-25. It was translated from Russian into English by Henry N. Michael and edited by Alexander Dolitsky in the *Fairy Tales and Myths of the Bering Strait Chukchi*, 1997, pp. 12-13. Reference to the personal name of a hero of the cosmogonic legend, in this case Tepkelin, is a rare exception for this masculine gender of oral transmission among the aboriginal people of the Russian Far North. In the Eskimo legend "Kanak and the Eagles" is found another version about the origin of the islands in the Bering Strait: the giant eagles and Kanak with his son, as the result of a duel, fall down into the sea, transforming into islands and reefs.

Inalik—(Yupik; the Chukchi adaptation is Inetlin) An island in the Bering Strait (Little Diomede Island, United States).

Inetlin—Little Diomede Island, in the Bering Strait, or Little Rotmanov Island, belongs to the United States.

Imaklik—(Yupik; lit. "located in the sea"; the Chukchi adaptation is Imeglin). An island in the Bering Strait (Big Diomede Island or Ratmanov Island belongs to Russia). In the past, the island served as a stopover for the Siberian Yupik Eskimos and Chukchi to the Alaskan Eskimos—for the latter, when traveling to the Chukchi Peninsula.

Imeglin—Big Diomede Island, in the Bering Strait, or Big Ratmanov Island, belongs to Russia. In the past, the island served as a stopover for the Siberian Yupik Eskimos and Chukchi to the Alaskan Eskimos—for the latter, when traveling to the Chukchi Peninsula.

Kayak—a closed canoe with a light wooden frame completely decked with the hides of sea mammals, principally walrus.

Lakhtak—a bearded seal. The largest true seal normally found in the sea adjacent to Alaska, Kamchatka, and Chukotka.

Yaranga—a barrel-roofed dwelling in the form of a tent with a frame of poles covered with reindeer hides among the nomads, or with walrus hides among the coastal dwellers.

Editor's note: The narrator did not describe an animal in the story. The illustrators, Tamara Semenova and Leigh Rust, took the liberty and artistic license to provide a creative image of this creature for readers based on their personal imaginations and interpretations of the story.

Editor's note: Scientists believe the islands of Inetlin and Imeglin were formed in the second millennium A.D, as the result of a cataclysmic geological event. In this story, the area's indigenous inhabitants appear to be recalling that event.

Образование пролива

Рассказал в 1948 г. житель села Яндагай Чукотского района Пакайка, 62 лет; записал и перевёл П.Я. Скорик. Сказка опубликована впервые в книге *Сказки и мифы народов Чукотки и Камчатки*, 1974:223-25. Указание на собственное имя героя космогонического предания (здесь— Тэпкэлин) является редким исключением для этого жанра устного творчества палеоазиатов. В эскимосском предании «Канак и орлы» даётся другая версия о происхождении островов в Беринговом проливе: орлы-великаны и Канак с сыном, упавшие в результате поединка в море, превратились в острова и рифы.

Инетлин—остров в Беринговом проливе (остров Крузенштерна, или Малый Диомид, США).

Имеглин—остров в Беринговом проливе (о-в Большой Диомид, или Ротманов, Россия). Этот остров с древнейших времён служил первоначальным пунктом морских поездок азиатских эскимосов и чукчей к аляскинским эскимосам, а последних — на Чукотку.

Каяк—охотничья лодка с легким деревянным каркасом, обтянутым тюленьей шкурой, и закрытым верхом. Гребец садился в люк и затягивался шнуром.

Лахтак—морской заяц (вид тюленя).

Яранга—наземное жилище в виде шатра с остовом из жердей, крытых оленьими шкурами (у кочевников) или моржовыми шкурами (у приморских жителей). *Яранги* приморских жителей строились с более сложным каркасом из балок и тонких жердей.

The Mouse and the Marmot

The tale was recorded by F. Tynetegyn and translated into Russian by Georgiy Melnikov, and published in Russian by Georgiy A. Menovshchikov in *Skazki i mify narodov Chukotki i Kamchatki* (Fairy Tales and Myths of the People of Chukotka and Kamchatka), 1974, pp. 336-37. It was translated from Russian into English by Henry N. Michael and edited by Alexander Dolitsky in *Fairy Tales and Myths of the Bering Strait Chukchi*, 1997, p. 106.

Мышка и евражка

Записал Ф. Тынэтэгын, перевёл Георгий И. Мельников. Сказка опубликована в книге *Сказки и мифы народов Чукотки и Камчатки*, 1974:336-37.

Akannykay—Bad Antlers

The story was narrated in 1948 by Ragtyn, age 36, an inhabitant of Lorino village in Chukotskiy region and recorded and translated into Russian by P. Skorik. It was published in Russian by Georgiy A. Menovshchikov in *Skazki i mify narodov Chukotki i Kamchatki* (Fairy Tales and Myths of the People of Chukotka and Kamchatka), 1974, pp. 338-43. The story was translated from Russian into English by Henry N. Michael and edited by Alexander Dolitsky in *Fairy Tales and Myths of the Bering Strait Chukchi*, 1997, pp. 108-110.

Akannykay—literally "Bad Antlers."

Matachgyrkynaynyn—"the son of a bad match," literally either "lewd matchmaker" or "male-dog matchmaker." The mention of a deer-like animal with dog-like paws occurs for the first time in Chukchi fairy tales about animals.

Аканныкай-плохорогонький

Рассказал в 1948 г. житель села Лорино Чукотского района Рагтын, 36 лет; записал и перевёл П.Я. Скорик. Сказка опубликована впервые в книге *Сказки и мифы народов Чукотки и Камчатки*, 1974:338-43.

Аканныкай—буквально «Плохорогонький».

Матачгыркынайнын—буквально «Сват-кобелище». Упоминание об оленеподобном звере с собачьими лапами отмечается впервые в чукотских сказках о животных.

FURTHER READING

Andersen, Hans Christian

1974   *The Complete Fairy Tales and Stories.* Translated by Eric Christian Haugaard. New York: Doubleday.

Bogoras, Waldemar

1901   The Chukchi of Northeastern Asia. *American Anthropologist* 3: 80-108.

1902   Folklore of Northeastern Asia as Compared with that of Northwestern America. *American Anthropologist* 4: 577-683.

1909   The Chukchee. *The Jesup North Pacific Expedition* 7. Memoirs of the American Museum of Natural History. Leiden-New York (Reprinted 1975, New York: AMS Press).

1910   Chukchee Mythology. *The Jesup North Pacific Expedition* 8(1). Memoirs of the American Museum of Natural History. Leiden-New York (Reprinted 1975, New York: AMS Press).

1913   The Eskimo of Siberia. *The Jesup North Pacific Expedition* 8(3). Memoirs of the American Museum of Natural History. Leiden/New York (Reprinted 1975, New York: AMS Press).

de Laguna, Frederica (ed.) and Dale DeArmond (illustrator)

1995   *Tales from the Dena: Indian Stories from the Tanana, Koyukuk, & Yukon Rivers.* Seattle & London: University of Washington Press.

Dolitsky, Alexander B. (ed.) and Henry N. Michael (translator)

1997   *Fairy Tales and Myths of the Bering Strait Chukchi.* Juneau: Alaska-Siberia Research Center, Publication No. 9.

2000   *Tales and Legends of the Yupik Eskimos of Siberia.* Juneau: Alaska-Siberia Research Center, Publication No. 11.

2002   *Ancient Tales of Kamchatka.* Juneau: Alaska-Siberia Research Center, Publication No. 12.

2008   *Spirit of the Siberian Tiger: Folktales of the Russian Far East.* Juneau: Alaska-Siberia Research Center, Publication No. 15.

Fitzhugh, William W. and Aaron Crowell (eds.)

1988   *Crossroads of Continents: Cultures of Siberia and Alaska.* Washington D.C.: The Smithsonian Institution Press.

Grimm, Jacob and Wilhelm

1987   *The Complete Fairy Tales of the Brothers Grimm.* Edited and translated by Jack Zipes. New York: Bantam.

Kerttula, Anna M.

2000   *Antler of the Sea: The Yup'ik and Chukchi of the Russian Far East.* Ithaca and London: Cornell University Press.

Menovshchikov, Georgiy A.

1974   *Skazki i mify narodov Chukotki i Kamchatki* (Fairy Tales and Myths of the People of Chukotka and Kamchatka). Moscow: Nauka.

Nagishkin, Dmitriy and Gennadiy Pavlishin

1980   *Amurskiye Skazki* (*Fairy Tales of the Amur*). Khabarovsk: Khabarovsk Press, Russia.

Tatar, Maria

2004   *The Annotated Brothers Grimm*. New York & London: W. W. Norton & Company.

Van Deusen, Kira

1999   *Raven and the Rock: Storytelling in Chukotka.* Seattle-London: University of Washington Press; Edmonton: Canadian Circumpolar Institute Press.

ABOUT THE AUTHOR/EDITOR

Alexander Dolitsky was born and raised in Kiev, in the former Soviet Union. He received an M.A. in history from Kiev Pedagogical Institute, Ukraine, in 1976; an M.A. in anthropology and archaeology from Brown University in 1983; and attended the Ph.D. program in anthropology at Bryn Mawr College from 1983 to 1985, where he was also a lecturer in the Russian Center.

In the U.S.S.R., he was a social studies teacher for three years and an archaeologist for five years at the Ukranian Academy of Sciences. In 1978, he settled in the United States after living one year in Austria and Italy. Dolitsky visited Alaska for the first time in 1981 while conducting field research for graduate school at Brown. He then settled in Alaska—first, in Sitka in 1985, and then in Juneau in 1986. From 1985 to 1987, he was the U.S. Forest Service archaeologist and social scientist. He was an Adjunct Assistant Professor of Russian Studies at the University of Alaska Southeast from 1985 to 1999; Social Studies Instructor at the Alyeska Central School, Alaska Department of Education and Yukon-Koyukuk School District from 1988 to 2006; and Director of the Alaska-Siberia Research Center (*see* www.aksrc.org) from 1990 to present. He has conducted approximately 30 field studies in various areas of the former Soviet Union (including Siberia), Central Asia, South America, Eastern Europe, and the United States (including Alaska).

Dolitsky has been a lecturer on the *World Discoverer*, *Spirit of Oceanus*, and *Clipper Odyssey* vessels in the Arctic and sub-Arctic regions. He was the Project Manager for the WWII Alaska-Siberia Lend-Lease Memorial erected in Fairbanks, Alaska, in 2006. Dolitsky is the founder and Program Manager of the "White Nights Festival of Russian Culture" that is held annually in Southeast Alaska.

He has published extensively in the fields of anthropology, history, archaeology, and ethnography in *Current Anthropology*, *Arctic*, *American Antiquity*, *Ultimate Reality and Meaning*, *Sibirica*, and in many other professional journals. His more recent books include: *Fairy Tales and Myths of the Bering Strait Chukchi*; *Tales and Legends of the Yupik Eskimos of Siberia*; *Ancient Tales of Kamchatka*; *Old Russia in Modern America: Russian Old Believers in Alaska*; *Allies in Wartime: The Alaska-Siberia Airway During World War II*; and *Spirit of the Siberian Tiger: Folktales of the Russian Far East*.

ABOUT THE ILLUSTRATOR
TAMARA SEMENOVA

Born and raised in Leningrad, Tamara Semenova is a well-known Saint Petersburg artist. Tamara's style is influenced by the Florentine School of the early Renaissance. Her canvases are full of light, energy, and emotion; they exhibit some mysterious power, symbolizing love and harmony.

As a small child, Tamara expressed her visions through art. Despite her mother's desire for her to study politics at the university, she entered Mukhina Institute of Arts and Design in Saint Petersburg. After graduation, she worked in Mozhaysky Aerospace Institute as one of the designers of the spaceship "Energy." In 1991, she continued her study of art in Perugia, Italy. On her return to Russia, she worked as a leading artist of the Institute of Arctic and Antarctic in Saint Petersburg.

In 1993, together with her husband Azat Mamedinov, she founded the International Art Festival Master Class, under the supervision of the Hermitage Museum and its director M.B. Piotrovsky. Today, it is one of the largest International Art Festivals in Saint Petersburg, annually hosting hundreds of artists from around the world.

In 1997, the Vatican invited artists from different countries to take part in a special event—painting God's Angels. The Angel painted by Tamara was so highly appreciated that it was exhibited in Krakow Cathedral in Poland, where John Paul II once served as a cardinal. The Angel then became a common thread in many of her works. Her painted Angels have soothed many troubled souls. Her works are to be found in museums and private collections in the United States, Russia, China, Italy, Austria, Ireland, Poland, Kazakhstan, Sweden, and Finland.

Tamara's art works have garnered many awards, including the United Nations' "Peacemaker of the Year 2008" medal. Tamara is often asked to exhibit her work worldwide and is available for private commissions, including portraiture.

ABOUT THE ILLUSTRATOR
LEIGH RUST

Leigh Rust was born and raised in Melbourne, Australia, and developed close ties with animals during his formative years. Some of his early memories include feeding an Asian Elephant and playing with monkeys. Over the past decade, after working as a comic illustrator and signwriter, his passion for wildlife has been rekindled as he has extended his skills into the realm of realist artwork.

He has been a member of the Australian Guild of Realist Artists since 2001, and last year collected two commendations in the national Australia Art Large competition.

He held his first solo exhibition in 2006, and followed that success with the formation of the Untamed Artist Network, a group of wildlife artists spanning the globe who share Leigh's passion for wildlife conservation and pledged to donate a portion of their profits to wildlife programs.

Leigh's giving nature also extends to other human beings. He had been an active participant in online forums, such as wetcanvas, showing his working methods and helping to nurture the skills of his fellow artists. His passion for teaching has led him to online art classes, in which he allows students to learn at their own pace in their own space. He has also earned a reputation as a talented demonstrator, sought out by many art shows around Australia.

In early 2008, Leigh worked with the Melbourne Zoo to present Twilight art demonstrations as part of the annual Twilight concert series.

Leigh has collected many awards throughout his career, and his work is held in private collections the world over.

He worked with Patrick Hedges in 2008 to create the *Tears of Leaves* exhibition, which was on display at Monarto Zoo, South Australia, from October 2008 to December 2008. The show was opened by Dr. Jane Goodall.

In 2009, two of Leigh's works made the finals of BBC's Wildlife Artist of the Year competition.

Leigh currently works on various art projects while teaching his growing legion of students in the ways of pastel.